Tony Scaduto was an investigative journalist for the *New York Post* for 20 years, and has been freelance since 1970. As a newspaper reporter, his specialities were the Mafia – who dominated the Brooklyn neighbourhood where he was brought up – and rock music. His approach to writing about the lives of superstars is that of a police reporter, which he once was. His philosophy is: 'Go out and interview everyone who will speak to you about your subject – even if your subject objects!'

Frank Sinatra

TONY SCADUTO

SPHERE BOOKS LIMITED
30/32 Gray's Inn Road, London WC1X 8JL

First published in Great Britain by Michael Joseph Ltd 1976
Copyright © Tony Scaduto, 1976
First Sphere Books edition 1977

Printed in Great Britain by
Hazell Watson & Viney Ltd
Aylesbury, Bucks

LIST OF ILLUSTRATIONS

Between pages 80 and 81

*All photographs by courtesy of Popperfoto, except number
16 which is by courtesy of Keystone Press*

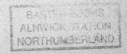

INTRODUCTION

I've been a Frank Sinatra fan since I was ten years old, when I froze in a line at the New York Paramount Theatre on New Year's Day, 1943. Surrounded by thousands of those dumb screaming girls that little boys normally run away from, I couldn't run. I just had to see Sinatra.

On Sinatra's first appearance at the Paramount – two days before I travelled up there escorted by older girls from my Brooklyn neighbourhood – Frank had been billed as an 'Extra Added Attraction' to sing a few songs with Benny Goodman, then the King of Swing. I didn't know it at the time, but on the day of his first appearance Goodman laconically introduced him this way: 'And now, Frank Sinatra.'

The roof promptly fell in. Sinatra later described what it felt like from the stage: 'The sound that greeted me was absolutely deafening. It was a tremendous roar ... I was scared stiff ... I couldn't move a muscle. Benny froze, too. He turned around, looked at the audience, and asked, "What the hell is that?" I burst out laughing and gave out with "For Me and My Gal".'

The roar shook Broadway for the next month. Frank had been but an extra in the Goodman holiday show, but when Goodman's engagement ended Sinatra stayed on, a star. 'The proclamation of a new era', *Life* magazine called it. But none of us needed *Life* to tell us; we had discovered Frankie, as we called him, on his earlier recordings with the Harry James band, especially the song 'All or Nothing at All'.

It was the following year, at the same Paramount, that the riots occurred. Again, I was there. Girls fainted and were carried out on stretchers. Girls fought over places in the line, were shoved through plate-glass windows, and again were carried away on stretchers. They – we – were absolutely insane over this skinny kid (he was actually 29) from Hoboken, New Jersey, a slum town across the Hudson River.

He was a true pop phenomenon. Almost a quarter of a century before the Beatles transformed our kids into screaming idiots, Sinatra created a mass hysteria in America, and then the world.

Like the bodyguard who once said he'd kill for Sinatra, his fans were tremendously loyal. I remember taking the subway up to the Paramount on Saturday afternoon to picket the Tommy Dorsey band. Sinatra had once sung with the Dorsey group, and the newspapers reported he was suing Dorsey because the band leader had forced Sinatra to sign a contract for almost half his earnings in return for permitting Frank to go out on his own as a solo act. We weren't going to permit Dorsey to earn a living until he freed our Frankie.

And we were thrilled when we heard on the fan club grapevine that Dorsey settled the suit only after a Mafia hoodlum put a gun to his head. The apparent truth – that Sinatra bought back his contract for about $50,000 – wasn't as sordidly glamorous, so we ignored that official version. All we cared about was that, as Frank put it, 'I now own myself' and that he had used the American way, guns and muscle, to reclaim that self.

But most of all we applauded Sinatra's conquest of Hollywood, professionally and sexually. The fan magazines never told us, but we knew from reading the raunchier gossip columnists that Sinatra was bedding practically every sex goddess in the film community. That, as one scandal sheet expressed it, the definition of the word *square* was any girl in Hollywood 'who hasn't been to bed with Frank Sinatra'. The skinny kid down the street was making out, fulfilling all our dreams. The boys' dreams, anyway; the girls, I suppose, had each of them to fantasize that they could become another Sinatra conquest.

I have to this day remained a fan of this man who has been the greatest popular singer and entertainer of our lifetime. But over the years, watching Sinatra as he broke up his first marriage in such a publicly boorish way, caroused with celluloid goddesses and sluts, punched people in the face or ordered the goons around him to beat them up, I often wondered whether some kind of gear had slipped inside the man. Perhaps it was some disruption of chemistry that made him behave so dreadfully to so many.

And yet I never thought about it very seriously. Not even in 1959 when I was assigned to investigate Sinatra's early background in the Hoboken slums where he was born and raised. I was one of a half-dozen reporters at the *New York Post* compiling information on Sinatra for a long series of articles. On my trips to Hoboken, I learned that many of his childhood friends had grown to dislike him, and they had many anecdotes to justify their attitude. But even as I reported my finding to my editors, I personally dismissed them as jealousy. Frank was not only a legend, but an idol of my childhood; one does not question too closely the dreams of childhood.

I remember defending Sinatra through the years. He was always page one news in America, and most of it was dreadful. If a New York City newspaper photographer charged that Sinatra tried to run him down with his limousine, I knew from personal experience that the photographer was ambitious, publicity-mad and untrustworthy, and I'd argue with friends that the incident probably never occurred at all, and if it had, it could not have been Sinatra's fault. When a newspaper columnist sued Sinatra for beating him up, I knew the columnist hated Sinatra and provoked the fight; Sinatra, I felt, acted properly in slugging the man, and I was sorry he hadn't knocked out the columnist's front teeth.

That myopia began to clear in 1974, when Sinatra threw his temper tantrum in Australia, creating an international incident which received more newspaper space than had the bombing of Cambodia. At first I defended Sinatra. Had he called Australian journalists whores and hookers? Well, he was probably correct; an Australian journalist friend had often used similar expressions to describe her colleagues. Did Frank refuse to bow to the demands of the press? Well, that was his right, for the press had never treated him too kindly.

But as the Siege of Sinatra continued in Sydney, I slowly realized my position was untenable and had been untenable for a couple of decades. After the Australian brawl, Maxine Cheshire, the Washington correspondent who was verbally attacked by Sinatra at a Nixon inaugural party in 1973 (he called her a 'two-dollar cunt'), said, 'The man is sick, he's schizophrenic. He's one of the greatest talents of this century, yet he is sick ... he's self-destructive.' I began to wonder about Sinatra. And then, during an argument one night with Stephanie Trudeau, an actress, singer, writer, and very dear friend, my defences began to crumble. She recounted incidents from his past which proved, she said, 'Sinatra is a violent, self-centred man who hates women.'

I stuck to what by now had become my last defence : 'He's behaved so badly over the years because reporters have always invaded his privacy, and usually printed lies about him.'

And Stephanie asked, 'Why don't you get the truth and write a book about him? Are you afraid of what you'll find inside your idol?'

'But Sinatra's been done dozens of times', I said rather lamely.

'No he hasn't. Not really. You've told me stories that've never been published from the time you went to Hoboken and talked to everybody. I bet you'll find a lot of fresh material.'

'Just finding a few new stories isn't enough. . . .'

'And you're Sicilian. Your father was. You grew up in the same kind of neighbourhood. You have the same kind of background. You can probably bring something very special to a book about him. Special insights. Or are you really afraid your idol is made of clay?'

A challenge I couldn't refuse. The result is this book, a close look inside my idol.

CHAPTER 1

So here's Frank Sinatra, who would later threaten to stab Mario Puzo with a fork because of his fictionalized portrait of a singer in *The Godfather*, a singer who could only have been Mr Sinatra. Here's Frankie sitting and chatting with the movie's director, Francis Ford Coppola, before filming started.

'I never liked exploiting the fictionalization of a man, any man – and I told him so', Coppola said later, recalling the conversation. 'I let him know I didn't like that part of the book and that I'd minimize it in the film. Sinatra was very appreciative.'

It must have been more than appreciation of Coppola's graciousness because Sinatra interrupted and said, 'I'd like to play the Godfather.'

Coppola doesn't tell us his reaction (in a *Playboy* interview in which he described this scene), but surely he was rather startled since it was known throughout Hollywood that Frankie was very very angry over what Puzo had written. And yet, Sinatra seemed genuinely excited about the prospect of playing Don Corleone: 'Let's you and me buy this goddamned book and make it ourselves', Sinatra said.

'Well, it sounds great, but. . . .'

The *but* no doubt included the fact that Paramount had already signed Marlon Brando (a pet Sinatra hate) for the role. Still, it makes a biographer wonder: Did Sinatra want the part because he believed it could bring him another Academy Award, or was it that, as some former friends believe, Sinatra actually thinks of himself as a Godfather running the lives of the men and women in his own unique show biz 'family'?

Those who were once part of the Sinatra circle and who, now that they've been dropped, have talked to me about this facet of Sinatra's quite complex personality, say they recognize it as part of Sinatra's fantasy world. But they're not certain *he* realizes it's a fantasy.

That fantasy is but a part of the unreal world Sinatra began to build around himself more than thirty years ago, when young girls fainted at the sight of him and mobbed him in the streets and no doubt dreamed of losing their virginity to him. And when reporters also mobbed him, asking how he felt about the girls who would tear the clothes off his back if they could, Sinatra preferred building up a certain kind of image that does come near to a fantasy.

'I was a slum kid', he used to say. He often recounted the time in Hoboken, that dock-side town in New Jersey that is so very much like Liverpool, when two policemen stopped him on the street because he was wearing a brand new suit. They suspected he had stolen it because Hoboken slum residents couldn't afford to clothe their children except in rummage sale specials. Sinatra insisted his mother had bought the suit for him but, he claimed, the police didn't believe him and they 'beat the stuffing out of me until I was a bleeding mess and my clothes were ruined'.

There were dozens of similar incidents in the Sinatra litany which he usually ended by saying that if he hadn't become a singer he would have been a gangster. In one story, Frank said his head had been cut open by a bottle in a gang fight. Another time, he said, a member of an enemy teen gang smashed him in the side of the head with a tyre chain. They were 'vicious gang wars', Sinatra told the reporters, and he still bore scars from them.

As late as 1961 he was telling English journalist Robin Douglas-Home, 'My old man thought that anyone who wanted to go into the music business must be a bum. So I picked up and left home for New York. I quit high school to do it, too.'

In truth, there were no gang wars in Sinatra's life. He was

beaten occasionally for he was small and brash and was always well dressed — 'a spoiled brat who got everything he wanted from his mother', one childhood friend from Hoboken remembered with undisguised envy – but Frank didn't run with any 'gang'. His uncle, Dominick Garaventi, a former professional fighter, told me years ago, 'There were no gang fights, like we know them. Just fighting, the way kids have always been fighting, and nobody every really got hurt by it.' And Uncle Dom didn't remember Frank getting beaten up by two cops. 'I'd know about that if it happened', he said.

Further, Sinatra's parents encouraged his singing after their initial negative reaction. His mother, Dolly, twisted arms to get him booked into small clubs as a vocalist, and it was she who persuaded a neighbourhood trio to take Frank on and become a quartet – Frank's first professional break.

But to Sinatra, either for the image he wanted to portray or the fantasy in which he enveloped himself so early, the Hoboken years took on a sinister aura. As if he'd seen too many bad movies with Jimmy Cagney and Pat O'Brien. For example, in talking about how music kept him from becoming a hood, Sinatra once said, 'You find that there are just as many angles to figure in being honest as there are in being crooked. If what you do is honest and you make it, you're a hero. If what you do is crooked and you make it, you're a bum. Me? I just grabbed a song.'

An actor who was once a member of Sinatra's old Rat Pack recently told me, 'Frank wants everybody to think he's a tough man. That's why he used to claim he grew up in the Hoboken slums and was always involved in gang wars, when he was really just another kid spoiled by his mother. That's why he likes all those hard-nosed guys around him, those Mafia types. And that's why he behaves like *Il Padrone*, the patron, the boss. You practically have to kneel and kiss his ring, like he's the Pope, or you're out. And when you're out with Frank, you're out with the world.'

It happened even to Sammy Davis, who possibly reveres Frank and fawns on him more than any other man in their very wide circle of influential men and women. Some years back, during a radio interview in Chicago, Davis had the effrontery to state : 'I love Frank, but there are many things he does that there is no excuse for . . . I don't care if you are the most talented person in the world. It does not give you the right to step on people and treat them rotten. This is what he does occasionally.'

As soon as Frank verified the rumours he'd heard about Davis's remarks, he got instant revenge. At the time, Davis was scheduled to begin work on *Never So Few,* playing a role that had been specially written into the script at Sinatra's request. The Davis part was promptly rewritten and it went to Steve McQueen. The penitent Davis tried for months to make amends to the Leader, without success. Finally, in one of his frequent acts of spontaneous generosity, Sinatra permitted Davis to apologize during a Miami benefit for retarded children and was reinstated in the inner circle. And there hasn't been a disparaging word from Davis since.

Davis was lucky; he is one of the few who have been forgiven by Sinatra. Frequently, an insult or a more serious wrong to Sinatra brings long-term revenge, the vendetta for which Frank is famous. Back in 1950, Sinatra's career was on a long downward slide for dozens of reasons, not least of which was that of his own self-destructive impulses during his pursuit of Ava Gardner. Mitch Miller of Columbia Records suggested that Frank record some up-tempo songs to keep up with new stars such as Eddie Fisher, Teresa Brewer, Frankie Laine, and other 'belters' who were cutting hit records. Miller, the new A&R man at Columbia, understood that teen-agers were buying more records than adults, and they would not listen to the old Sinatra. They were buying a counterfeit white version of the black rhythm and blues (Miller was the major and most successful promoter of the white ripoff of that style).

But Sinatra's efforts to keep up with changing tastes fell absolutely flat. The downward curve of his record sales which had begun more than a year earlier continued, and by 1951 his average sales fell below 10,000 copies of each release. He was more concerned about chasing Ava than about anything else in life, and his voice and career suffered for it. Frank at one time placed the blame for the destruction of his career squarely where it belonged – on his own shoulders. 'I was mixed up', he said of those days. 'My singing was affected and I knew it.'

And yet, after he won the Academy Award for his role as Private Maggio in *From Here To Eternity* and once more reigned as Hollywood's King (a title which, along with Pope and Leader, Sinatra graciously accepted as only his due), he suddenly discovered the main and only reason for his years of decline : Mitch Miller. In September, 1956, after apparently nursing a deep anger at Miller for years, Sinatra fired off a telegram to a congressional committee investigating the television industry.

'Before Mitch Miller's arrival at Columbia', Sinatra wrote, 'I found myself enjoying a freedom of selection of material, a freedom which I may modestly say resulted in a modicum of success for me. Suddenly, Mr Miller, by design or coincidence, began to present many inferior songs, all curiously bearing the BMI (Broadcast Music, Inc.) label. Before Mr Miller's advent on the scene, I had a successful recording career which quickly went into decline. Rather than continue a frustrating battle, I chose to take my talents elsewhere. It is now a matter of record that since I have associated myself with Capitol Records, a company free of broadcasting affiliations, my career is again financially, creatively, and artistically healthy.'

In his telegram, Sinatra quite conveniently ignored the fact that his career began falling apart before Miller took over at Columbia, that his records weren't selling, that in fact he did not leave his record company out of frustration but because Columbia cancelled his contract. He completely forgot that film companies had stopped offering him roles and his own agency, Music Corporation of America, dropped him from its list. Frank also ignored the fact that 95 per cent of the songs he recorded under Miller were not BMI songs. All of Sinatra's own mistakes suddenly became focused on one man Mitch Miller, a conspirator out to destroy Sinatra's career.

Sinatra's desire for revenge against Miller led to a similar telegram a year later to a Senate committee investigating payola in the recording industry. This time, Sinatra charged that Miller had received kickbacks from songwriters whose songs he recorded. Nothing much ever came of the charges except further proof of Frank's ability to carry on a vendetta for years.

Long after he had made these accusations, Sinatra met Miller in a Las Vegas hotel. Miller walked up to him, hand outstretched, and almost pleaded, 'Let bygones be bygones.' Sinatra's hard blue eyes stared at Miller's hand for a moment. Then he turned and walked away, muttering an epithet that has been lost to history because reporters who wrote of it could only say he used several 'unprintable words'.

'Frank's just like me,' Sinatra's mother, Dolly, once said. 'Cross him once and he never forgets.'

Frank seldom forgives an insult and he carries his hatreds around for years, sometimes even after the object of that hatred has been lowered into the grave. His memory for insults is sharpest when the person he's hating is a writer or columnist, as it usually is.

Gossip columnist Dorothy Kilgallen once criticized Frank for some misbehaviour or other. He promptly placed her on his 'Sinatra list', a drop-dead list that in some circles is to be feared more than death itself. When Sinatra opened at the Sands, the gambling joint in Las Vegas in which he had a financial interest, he went into a twenty-minute diatribe about Miss Kilgallen, concentrating on her very small chin which made her look like a chipmunk and her very large capacity for alcohol. When a couple of his associates warned him that he was going too far, that he should avoid personal attacks and concentrate on what they considered her lack of professional integrity, Frank cut them out of his group. Sinatra then sent Miss Kilgallen a tombstone. No engraving on it – the message was more than obvious.

A couple of years later Miss Kilgallen did die rather suddenly. Never a man to compromise with his feelings, even when the object of his emotions died, Frank remarked, 'Well, I guess I got to change my whole act.'

Unfortunately, Sammy Davis never did describe, from his insider's vantage point, precisely how Sinatra steps on people and treats them 'rotten'. Frank's attacks upon journalists and photographers are well known, and some inside incidents, such as throwing a ketchup bottle at a friend for no valid reason, have leaked out of the King's court. But it is in Frank's treatment of his women that Davis's remarks take on a special meaning.

Frank had been married to Mia Farrow only four weeks when he opened an engagement at the Sands. Mia was sitting at a ringside table, of course. Between his songs, Frank began a patter about this unusual marriage between the 50-year-old King of Hollywood and the 20-year-old whose short haircut made her look like a young boy. (In fact, Ava Gardner, when told about the marriage, cracked, 'I always knew Frank always wanted a boy with a cunt.') A columnist who was at that opening night recalls : 'Frank grinned when he made the crack and I'm sure he meant it as a joke. He told his audience, "Maybe you wondered why I finally got married. Well, I finally found a broad I can cheat on." Mia didn't get the joke. Neither did I. She was sitting at her table with the boss of the Sands, and she looked stunned. She started to cry just a little bit. She was too cool a lady to get up and walk out, to let everyone see the hurt she felt. But you could tell she was badly hurt. Not only the crack about cheating, but that word *broad*. She hated that word. It's Frank's favourite.'

That incident occurred a decade ago. Is it possible, I asked all of those I interviewed in my attempt to understand the man behind the headlines, that Sinatra has changed in his attitude toward women now that he's entering his sixth decade? Not one bit, from all I've been able to learn.

When Sinatra took his entourage with him on that infamous Australian trip in 1974, one member of the party was Barbara Marx, the 48-year-old former model and Vegas showgirl who's been hoping, and it now seems that she may be successful, to become the fourth Mrs Frank Sinatra. One of Barbara's friends who was on that trip recalls, 'They had broken up before Australia and she had just been allowed back, but it was obvious to everyone that she was just about being tolerated by Frank. She kept saying, "I'm just on trial here. . . ." Sinatra's crowd has a Pain in the Ass Award that they give out every week. And Barbara said to me at one point, "If I'm not careful I'm going to get the Pain in the Ass of the *Year* Award."

'One night we were all having a drink in a restaurant very late and Barbara decided to go off to bed. She went over to say good night to Frank, who was sitting at a table talking to Jilly Rizzo and Pat Henry, his two most loyal followers. She didn't want to interrupt the conversation so she just leaned over and kissed him on the cheek. He seemed to go mad. "What the *hell* do you think you're *doing*?" he shouted in a really loud voice. "Don't you *ever dare* interrupt me when I'm talking to my friends." Barbara just slunk away. That kind of public humiliation was going on all the time.'

But Barbara takes it, friends say, because she broke up her marriage to be Frank's woman, and if he dumps her, even now, she will feel that at her age it's all over for her.

'Being a Sinatra woman isn't easy', the friend who was in Australia with them continues. 'Barbara spends hours in her bedroom getting ready for the simplest outing, even a shopping trip with the girls. Sinatra likes his women well groomed, and that takes a lot of time. The women are expected to seek their own place in the pecking order of the entourage, and any woman's place, even the one living with him, isn't very high up.

'Still, she looks pretty good. Kind of a Dina Merrill type. But she probably wears too much makeup. One day on the trip the makeup man who was travelling with us did her up and she looked sensational. I asked him what he put on her and he said it was more a question of what he took off.'

From the evidence available, Barbara was devoting much time to looking beautiful long before she became involved with Sinatra. When she was still married to her last husband, her third, Zeppo Marx of the Marx Brothers, a guest at a party told Zeppo that his wife looked exceptionally beautiful that evening. Zeppo retorted, 'She should. She works on it hard enough.'

Barbara met Zeppo in Las Vegas, where she was a showgirl and getting somewhat old for the role. She was, friends say, intelligent enough to understand that her good looks would fade and she'd be just another ex-showgirl bouncing around in a desert town filled with such women, and that realization undoubtedly played some part in her decision to marry Zeppo, who is a quarter of a century older than she.

The home Zeppo took her to, overlooking the Tamarisk Golf Course in Palm Springs, California, was just a few doors down from Sinatra's compound. Zeppo and Frank had been close friends for years, and now Barbara became a part of the Sinatra circle, attending the parties he constantly threw in Palm Springs, Beverly Hills, or Vegas. She and Zeppo were also included in a lot of Sinatra family dinners, with Frank's ex-wife Nancy and their children. At first, as far as Frank was concerned, Barbara was simply another good-looking woman married to a friend.

But that began to change in the winter of 1968, when Vice President-elect Spiro Agnew came to Palm Springs as the hero of the Republican Governors' Convention (those were the days before it was disclosed that Agnew had been a crook getting rich in the Maryland governor's office and had later continued to accept bribes in his White House office). Agnew liked to play tennis, and he liked to play with pretty women. Barbara Marx played a lot of tennis, both for the sport and for the healthy exercise. When one of Agnew's assistants, arriving in town a few days early to set things up for the boss, asked around about the chances of finding a couple of pretty women to play tennis with Agnew, Barbara was one of those recommended. A doubles match took place, with Barbara as Agnew's partner and, says a member of the Racquet Club, 'the Vice President had such a smashing time that a lot of other matches took place.'

The on-court relationship between Barbara and Agnew, and the dinners and drinks at Ruby Dunes Restaurant, later led to gossip and to a few column items suggesting that Barbara had pretended to leave Zeppo for Frank Sinatra, but it was all a ruse to hide the fact that she was really Agnew's girlfriend.

The rumour took on a great deal of weight because Agnew and his wife, after being house guests of Bob Hope during that first visit, began staying at Sinatra's home on future visits. It was larger and more secluded than Hope's, assuring the Agnews plenty of space and privacy, the official story went. But the gossips began to gossip even more, ignoring the fact that Frank and Spiro had become friendly long before the Republican convention voted him vice-presidential candidate. Sinatra was privately known as Agnew's 'sponsor' and had been heard to say, 'I'm going to make him Vice President.'

With Agnew as a frequent house guest – often without his wife and family – Sinatra began to see Barbara Marx in a different light. She had taken over the planning of Agnew's tennis and golf matches, and he obviously enjoyed her company and relied on her a great deal. So Sinatra began to call on her to be the hostess at parties he gave for Agnew.

'He was the town's most generous host and he needed a hostess to compliment him', one of Barbara's friends says. 'Barbara stepped in. And Frank began to think of her as an asset – not only as a beautiful woman, but one who was charming and intelligent and who turned on the Vice President of the United States. I'm sure Frank didn't think of this consciously, but don't forget he had been close to the seat of power with John Kennedy until Bobby Kennedy messed him up, and now he was close to the seat of power with Agnew. Barbara was very useful to him. And they grew very close.'

So close that Barbara moved out of her house and into Sinatra's. Since then she has been Frank's woman, living in his home, travelling with him to Europe, the only woman he's been seen with publicly except for a rare date with Jackie Kennedy or some other old friend.

For a couple of years her friends have predicted Frank would marry her, especially since she divorced Zeppo and agreed to what must be the world's record low alimony for those 'circles – only $1,500 a month for ten years, or until she remarries. As one friend told a reporter, 'The settlement is the tip that she'll marry Frank. She's too shrewd to have left Zeppo for that kind of settlement unless she knew exactly what her next move would be.'

At the time of this book's going to press, rumours of Frank and Barbara's engagement were confirmed. But will they marry? She has two problems to face: Hollywood insiders claim that the reason she fell from Sinatra's favour for a time, is that Sinatra's lawyer, Mickey Rudin, doesn't like Barbara and makes no secret of the fact. Rudin, it's said, is the real power in the Sinatra crowd. And he makes it clear he thinks Barbara is dangerous to have around because he believes she isn't very bright.

An even greater hurdle between Barbara and marriage to Frank is Dolly Sinatra, who lives in a house next door to her son. Dolly has always frowned on Frank's affair with Barbara. As she once angrily remarked, 'Aren't there enough women in the world without my son taking his best friend's wife?'

One of Sinatra's bodyguards once told a writer, 'I'd kill for him.' The man actually meant it. Among the men and women whose lives revolve around him, Sinatra inspires a loyalty that is fierce and sometimes vicious. Sinatra wants it that way. He demands it. That's part of the Sicilian in him. He is the wealthiest, most powerful, famous and talented man in show business, and he seems to believe he's automatically entitled to the unquestioning loyalty and respect that every *padrone* commands.

Frequently, Sinatra behaves as if he is indeed the Godfather, as if the lives of everyone around him must automatically be bent to his own needs and wishes. Comedian Pat Henry recently talked about Sinatra. During that brief interview, Henry related an anecdote whose main point – that the snap of Sinatra's finger is equal to a command from the Lord – never seems to have occurred to him as it never seems to occur to anyone else in Frank's circle.

'You never know what he has in store for you', said Henry. 'For instance, one time when I was at my home in New York, he invited me out to dinner. I told my wife I was going and she complained, "You told me you were too tired to go out and get me cigarettes, but you'll go out with Frank."

·'I promised to get her cigarettes on the way home. But after I got to the restaurant, Frank said he wanted me to see a new plane a friend of his had bought. So, before I knew it, we were off to the airport. We went up in the plane and we'd been flying for about two hours when I said, "Frank, the plane works okay, now let's go back." Frank looked at me and said, "Oh, I forgot to tell you, Pat, we're going to England for five days." Believe me it wasn't easy explaining to my wife over long distance from London that she'd have to go out and get her own cigarettes.'

Sinatra is famous for capers of that kind, forcing friends to drop everything because he is lonely and needs company. Practically every one of his friends who have talked about Frank, including those still in his group, have related how he will call in the middle of the night and insist they join him on a lark of some kind. All such anecdotes describe the event as a lark and no one ever seems to ask, 'Do I have a choice?'

Frank Sinatra is one of those men who have long been called, in Sicilian tradition, *uomini respettati,* men of respect. Men who are simultaneously majestic and humble, men who are loved and feared by all, men who are generous to those deserving of generosity and ferocious toward those who have committed a wrong.

Sinatra's generosity is enormous. He spends about $50,000 a year on gifts for his friends. At Christmas, he personally selects presents for his friends and members of their families, always remembering their favourite jewellery, favourite colours, the sizes they wear.

His generosity is also impulsive. He once heard that some children in Arizona were forced to walk long distances to school because there was no bus to carry them. He bought them a bus. Another time Sinatra sent his private jet liner to New York to bring a young cerebral palsy victim back to the West Coast after reading that the family's mini-bus had been stolen. A few years back, the house of one of Sinatra's musician friends was destroyed in a Los Angeles mud slide and his wife was killed. Frank rushed to his aid, finding a new home for the musician, paying hospital bills, then personally taking charge of furnishing the new home, down to replacing silverware, glasses, linens, and even buying the man new clothing.

Yet on the same day that Frank quietly spends thousands to help someone in trouble, he can explode in a violent rage because he believes he's been slighted or insulted, or because one of his aids has made a minor mistake. For example, one night one of Sinatra's minions brought him a frankfurter with ketchup on it. Sinatra doesn't like ketchup. He picked up the ketchup bottle and threw it at the man.

Perhaps in Sicily's dim past the men of respect were honest and fair, village Solomons, but over the last century or so being a man of respect has come to mean being a man of the Mafia. In Hoboken, in the Little Italies of every American city, as in Palermo and Partinico and every Sicilian town and village, *uomini respettati* and *mafiosi* are now absolutely synonymous.

It is, I know, quite easy for young men growing up in an area where Robin Hood lives to adopt for themselves such romantic concepts and to play-act at being men of respect. In my own childhood in Brooklyn, two decades after Sinatra's youth and in a less insulated Italian community, when we played cops and robbers, the robbers were the heroes, the cops were the bums. We fought most often over which of us would play the role of one on our neighbours, Don Giuseppe Profaci, at that time the most powerful *mafioso* in the nation. Had our parents known of our fantasies, we would have been thoroughly whipped and locked in our rooms for weeks.

Somehow, Sinatra doesn't seem to have ever shaken off that fantasy. 'I think', Bing Crosby once remarked, 'Sinatra's always nurtured a secret desire to be a hood.' In his low-key way, Crosby – who was artificially forced into the role of Sinatra's rival during radio's 'Battle of the Baritones' in the Forties and who came to know Sinatra well during their years in Hollywood – has come as close as anyone in getting to the core of Sinatra's personality: 'a secret desire to be a hood', not any old hood, but the Godfather himself.

Although it was seldom mentioned in the early days, when

Sinatra the Phenomenon was written about almost solely by reporters for the gossip columns and fan magazines, Frank has always had a coterie of hoods around him. Even thirty years ago, one of Sinatra's friends was telling E. J. Kahn, an early Sinatra biographer, 'In a way, Frank's still a little boy who likes to play cops and robbers. These characters (the hoods) latch themselves onto him and become paternal and possessive toward him. They are always looking out to see that nothing happens to Frankie, and it makes him happy to think they're tough hombres.'

A year or so after that, Sinatra received a great deal of unfavourable publicity when it was revealed that he had travelled to Havana to spend a little time with Charlie 'Lucky' Luciano, the deported real-life Godfather who was attempting to get back into the United States and who had called all the leaders of the American Mafia to a series of business conferences. What Sinatra was doing in Cuba in the company of dozens of *mafiosi*, he's never deigned to explain.

Gay Talese saw one aspect of Sinatra's Godfather syndrome long before Puzo's book made *godfather* a household word and a cliché. On assignment from *Esquire* magazine in 1965, Talese followed Sinatra around, observing the man and his setting. He wrote about an evening at Jilly's bar, Sinatra's favourite watering hole in New York: 'Some of Sinatra's close friends, all of whom are known to the men guarding Jilly's door, do manage to get an escort into the back room. But once they are there, they too must fend for themselves. On the particular evening, Frank Gifford, the former football player, got only seven yards in three tries. Others who had somehow been close enough to shake Sinatra's hand did *not* shake it; instead they just touched him on the shoulder or sleeve, or they merely stood close enough for him to see them and, after he'd given them a wink of recognition or a wave or a nod or called out their names (he has a fantastic memory for first names), they would then turn and leave. They had checked in. They had paid their respects.'

Thinking about the ritual Talese had observed, my mind flashed back to the evening I drove down to New York's

Little Italy to have dinner with friends. After parking the car, I walked toward the restaurant and passed a storefront with lettering on the front door that read 'Alto Knight's Social Club. Private.' The windows had been painted black so that casual passersby could not observe the interior. But it was a hot summer night and the front door was open. Sitting at a small table, flanked by two burly men, was Vito Genovese, at that time the Boss of All Bosses of the Mafia. His attitude seemed to be that of a Mussolini, receiving homage from his sycophants. And as I watched, briefly, for it would have been indiscreet to gaze too long, one *mafioso* was summoned by a curt nod from Don Vitone and stepped out of the line of men against one wall. He walked to the table with the shuffle of a slave, leaned over, and kissed Genovese's hand.

Frank's eldest child, Nancy, has said of him, 'He has everything, he cannot sleep, he gives nice gifts, he is not happy, but he would not trade, even for happiness, what he is. . . .

'He is a piece of our past, but only *we* have aged, he hasn't . . . *We* are dogged by domesticity, he isn't . . . *We* have compunctions, he doesn't . . . It is *our* fault, not his. . . .

'Men follow him, imitate him, fight to be near him . . . There is something of the locker room, the barracks about him. . . .

'He believes you must play it big, wide, expansively. The more open you are, the more you take in, your dimensions deepen, you grow, you become more what you are – bigger, richer. . . .

'He is better than anybody else, or at least they think he is, and he has to live up to it.'

To even hope to begin to understand this man without compunctions, one must attempt to understand the place of the popular artist in our society. Whether he's a singer, musician, painter, or actor, the pop artist is invariably dependent on those men who control the sale of his talent. Obviously. But what is not so obvious is that, during the earliest years of an artist's career, he is often treated as if he were no more than another piece of excrement on the dung heap. He is forced to audition for men and women whose attitude is that of the American generals in Vietnam keeping a body count. Take your slab of meat and your talent onto the stage for sixty or ninety seconds, after waiting in a cattle-line for three hours, then get cut short: 'Next!' Land a job in a show or a club and have your ego destroyed and the props cut from under you by hysterical directors and callous stage managers shoving talent around like inanimate pieces on a chess board. And on and on.

The slab-of-meat-on-a-butcher-block attitude is seen in its most abominable form in the remarks of producer-director George Sidney, speaking about Ava Gardner. In 1941 Sidney's job was to select new starlets for MGM. A screen test of Ava, made by studio executives in New York, was sent to Hollywood and viewed by Sidney. Thirty years later, he recalled for Ava's biographer, Charles Higham, that after seeing Ava's test he cried to an assistant, 'Tell New York to ship her out! She's a good piece of merchandise!'

Every artist is very vulnerable. Each time he gets out there to perform he is laying himself wide open, and down deep there is always an intense fear of rejection. The artist is never certain whether he's *really* good enough. Every performer goes through periods of self-doubt, and Sinatra was no exception. During his conflicts with Dorsey, he thought seriously of quitting and seeking another line of work. Even at the height of his fame and power, after winning the Oscar for *Eternity* and making the most spectacular 'comeback' in entertainment history, Sinatra could tell friends, 'I'm no good.' He could leave columnist Joe Hyams with the impression that he was 'frightened' and 'expecting to be cut down from the heights at any moment'. Frank told Hyams. 'I'm always bucking the American game. "He's on top now. Knock him off." People root for you going up so they can knock you off later.'

Most dreadful of all to the popular artist is that the money men of the industry, the no-talents who care only about the bottom line of the ledger books and who control industry treasuries, understand these weaknesses, these fears, these self-doubts that plague the artist, and they sadistically take advantage of them.

An example? Frank Sinatra, at the depth of his career, desperately wanted to play the role of Maggio in *Eternity*. He was forced to *beg* studio boss Harry Cohn not for the role but for a screen test, even after having made eleven feature films. Cohn told Frank he wasn't an actor and he wouldn't be able to handle the role; he implied Frank was washed up and might even hurt the film; he seemed to take great delight in reminding Sinatra that he was professionally down in the pits. Later, another executive gave Frank the test, and when Cohn and his people saw Frank's sensitive acting, they immediately hired him. Frank got paid only scale, about $8,000, roughly $142,000 less than he had been getting for a film. And then Cohn went around boasting about *his* brilliant decision to put Frank in the film.

No wonder, then, that Sinatra, Brando, Gardner. Monroe, and so many others who have been treated as 'merchandise' will, once they've attained stardom, seem to become Frankenstein monsters, demanding enormous prices for their services and incredible privileges and percentages in their contracts. Although behaving like prima donnas, they are actually seeking revenge. According to one actor, who had become a star after years of fighting to be recognized by the men who control the Broadway theatre, 'The greatest thing about making it is that I can get *revenge*. I can tell the David Merricks of this world to pay me a million bucks or go fuck themselves, and the fucking themselves part is what I really mean.' No wonder Sinatra could say, as he did after winning his Oscar, 'I did it all myself.' Or, at another time, during an argument with a press agent who shouted that Sinatra was dependent on the public, Frank could cry, 'I am not! I have talent! I am dependent only on myself.'

The newspapers and magazines attacked Sinatra for that attitude, insisting he had help every step of the way to the top and couldn't have done it alone. They were wrong. Despite all the people who worked on *Eternity* with Sinatra, despite everyone who helped him in the years he was struggling as a band singer, Sinatra, like every real artist, did make it himself. Without his talent, without the drive, the ambition, the almost junkie-need to make it, no amount of help from anyone else could have made him a star.

Yet from the moment Frank found himself in the enviable position of getting paid thousands of dollars a performance (where once he sang for no more than car fare to radio stations from which he had wrangled fifteen-minute daily vocalizing slots) almost everyone who was ever introduced to him during the early years began taking credit for his success. In truth, his own determination and most of all his own talent, stand out above everything and everyone else. For about two years he learned his craft by singing eighteen times a week in New York City radio studios – at dawn, at noon, and at five o'clock in the afternoon – and then performing at the Rustic Cabin in New Jersey in the evening. It was a grinding schedule, but Frank kept on with it because his voice was being trained by constant use and because he knew the only way to escape from that lowest level of pop entertainment was to be heard by as many people as possible, to develop a following, and, perhaps, be heard by people in the industry who could offer him better jobs.

The first such offer came in June, 1939, when Frank was approaching 25 and had been singing professionally for about six years. Harry James, who had left Benny Goodman's band a few months earlier to form one of his own, was searching for a vocalist. He had heard about the 'skinny kid' at the Rustic Cabin who knew how to handle a ballad and who had developed a small but impassioned following of young women. James went out to have a look. 'I liked Frank's way of taking a lyric', James later said, 'and I went back the following night with my manager and we signed him for $75 a week.'

During the six months Sinatra was with the James band, he recorded several songs that went relatively unnoticed, including 'All or Nothing at All' which sold only about 8,000 copies in its first year (but sold more than a million when it was reissued in 1943, after both Sinatra and James had made it). But back then, in 1939, this first evidence of Sinatra's remarkable ability to take a pop ballad and make it sound as if he really *meant* the words he was singing, had an important effect on his career.

Again, it must be noted that it was Sinatra's voice, Sinatra's phrasing, Sinatra's sensitivity that touched a listener, that brought the next step upward. The publisher of 'All or Nothing at All' played the James-Sinatra record for Tommy Dorsey one day, hoping to persuade Dorsey to record the song and make it the hit that the new James band had failed to do. According to a song plugger who was there, 'Dorsey just sat there taking in this vocal. It seemed to intrigue him. He liked this guy Sinatra.' At the same time, Dorsey had heard reports about Sinatra's effect on his audiences, even on professionals. One of these professionals, a man who was music supervisor for CBS in Chicago and who knew that Dorsey was looking for a new male vocalist, asked Dorsey, 'Have you heard the skinny kid who's singing with Harry James? He's nothing to look at, but he's got a sound. First time I heard him, my back was to the bandstand. But when the kid started taking a chorus I had to turn around. I couldn't resist going back the next night to hear him again. He's got something besides problems with acne. Harry can't be paying him much. Maybe you can take him away.'

Never one to let ethical considerations stand in the way of business, Dorsey did just that. He took Sinatra away from the James band with an offer of twice the salary and a much wider audience because of his own band's popularity. At the same time he practically held up Sinatra's predecessor, Jack Leonard, who wanted to go out as a single act; he forced Leonard to sign, in return for a release from the Dorsey band, a personal management contract that gave Dorsey about 30 per cent of Leonard's gross earnings for the next ten years. Dorsey would pull the same deal on Sinatra a couple of years later.

Jo Stafford, then one of the Pied Pipers, the vocal quartet in the Dorsey group, remembers Frank's first performance: 'We were onstage when Tommy announced Frank's first appearance. As Frank came up to the mike I just thought "Hmmm, kinda thin." But by the end of eight bars I was thinking "This is the greatest sound I've ever heard." But he had more. Call it talent. You knew he couldn't do a number badly.'

In May, 1941, Sinatra came in first in *Billboard*'s annual survey of who the college kids were listening to. At the end of the year, *Down Beat* confirmed Sinatra's rapidly growing popularity by announcing he had displaced his rival and idol, Bing Crosby, as best male vocalist. And in January, 1942, Sinatra was chosen by the readers of *Metronome* as the best male band singer of the preceding year, making him the unanimous choice of the three major music papers in America.

Some of the songs he recorded with Dorsey, including 'This Love of Mine' (for which Frank wrote the lyrics) and 'I'll Never Smile Again', were among the best vocal recordings of the Big Band era, and also had an incredibly huge play on the nation's jukeboxes and radio stations. While most band singers of the day sounded as if they were being smothered by the musicians and were no more than appendages required by an audience which demanded singing, Sinatra rose above the band and at the same time sounded an integral part of it, almost another instrument taking its solo.

Sinatra learned a great deal from Dorsey, and despite his later resentment toward the man, he acknowledged the debt. 'Tommy taught me everything I knew about singing', Frank has said. 'He was my real education.' Most of all, Sinatra says, he learned breath control from Dorsey. He observed that Dorsey could play through long musical passages without sounding as if he were taking a breath. Frank stared at the trombonist night after night and finally discovered Dorsey was breathing through 'a sneak pinhole in the corner of his mouth, not an actual pinhole but a tiny place where he was breathing . . . In the middle of a phrase, while the tone was still being carried through the trombone, he'd take a quick breath and play another four bars with that breath.' Dorsey's trombone had a long flowing sound, rich and velvety, and Sinatra adapted the technique by learning to breathe through his nose during a long note. It gave his singing the unique flowing quality which continues to provoke listeners today.

But in his sentimental comments about Dorsey, made in 1961 while recording a tribute album called *I Remember Tommy*, Sinatra could hardly have stated what he must have really felt: Other singers had worked with Dorsey, had picked up tricks from him, had grown more professional from the experience, but only Sinatra became *the* Sinatra.

From the very beginning Sinatra believed the popular song was a vehicle for the projection of feelings – as did blues singers and jazzmen – and Frank completely devoted himself to making his songs instruments of self-expression. From the many jazzmen he came into contact with during his six months with James and his two years with Dorsey, he understood that a really good musician tries to bring something extra to music. He sought out the meaning of each song, working particularly hard on enunciation and word shading, and concentrating on breath control. Like a boxer in training, Frank began to swim and run, expanding the capacity of his lungs to the point where, with a single breath, he could suck in about 40 per cent more air than the average person. This, and having learned to breathe through his nose while singing, gave his voice its very special quality. (It is a measure of the man's talent that his 1973 back-from-retirement album, *Ol' Blue Eyes is Back*, is the finest he has ever recorded and fully demonstrates all the qualities that had made Sinatra's voice so exceptional more than thirty years earlier.)

Certainly Frank learned a few things from Dorsey, but he became Sinatra because he worked at it. And in turn his vocalizing helped to make the Dorsey band one of the most popular in the country.

But not quite the most popular, which grated on the enormous Dorsey ego. In the *Down Beat* poll in which Sinatra was number one vocalist, the Dorsey band placed second to Benny Goodman; worse still, Dorsey personally placed down on the list behind Artie Shaw, Harry James, and Benny Goodman in the instrumental soloist division. A shrewd businessman, Dorsey had the best recording contract in the industry, yet that first place in popularity continued to elude him while Sinatra's popularity kept rising. To put it more bluntly than most writers of the day ever did, Dorsey was jealous of Sinatra's popularity and reacted in mean, occasionally vicious, ways.

Friction between Sinatra and Dorsey grew during 1942, when Dorsey realized that the song pluggers who had always tried to peddle their wares to him now checked Frank's reaction first. They knew that if one of their songs became a Sinatra number, rather than part of the Pied Pipers' repertoire or a band number, it would sell a lot more records. Axel Stordahl, then one of Dorsey's arrangers, later said of the growing conflict, 'After a while it was not Tommy's show but Frank's.'

And then Dorsey's recording company, Victor, contributed to the conflict. Dorsey's record labels had always contained only his name and the notation 'Vocal Chorus'. Then, with hit after hit clearly attributable to the man singing the vocal chorus, and with thousands of letters asking the name of the vocalist, Victor executives suggested that Sinatra's name be put on the labels of all recordings in which he sang. At first Dorsey refused, but then he gave in: Sinatra's name could be used, but in the smallest type available. The type kept getting larger, however, and Dorsey more upset.

Soon Frank was asking to make solo records, under his own name and with his own choice of songs. Dorsey again objected that Frank was 'his' singer and refused to allow it. Sinatra insisted. Victor executives put the pressure on. Dorsey finally gave in. On 15th March 1942, Sinatra cut his first two solo sides, 'Night and Day' and 'The Night We Called It a Day'. But what Sinatra was not told until after the studio sessions was that his records would be released on the Bluebird subsidiary label, not the Victor label. Bluebird records sold at less than half the price of Victor records, and the company seldom promoted the minor label. That had been Dorsey's price for capitulating to Sinatra's demand to make his own records: 'Give him rope and let him hang himself with a few failures', as one Victor executive put it years later. But Sinatra's records sold remarkably well for the label; Frank used the rope to climb even farther.

Finally, Dorsey received some disturbing news from a

press agent who had been sent out on the road ahead of the band to drum up publicity. Everywhere he went, the flack reported to Tommy, journalists were more interested in Sinatra than in Dorsey or his group.

By that summer Sinatra decided he was ready to step out on his own, but Dorsey and his business manager had Sinatra under a five-year contract, and he'd fulfilled less than three years. They agreed to release him only if Sinatra signed a new contract giving them over 43 per cent of his *gross* earnings for the next ten years. Sinatra signed. 'He would have given anybody a piece of him then,' a friend later said.

Frank finally broke away from Dorsey in September, 1942. During the next twelve months he earned almost $200,000 – an enormous sum for a pop singer in those days. But of that amount he probably kept less than $50,000 before taxes because of cuts taken by Dorsey, booking and press agents, and several others who had staked a claim on him. The cuts came out of Sinatra's gross earnings as did travel expenses and the cost of arrangements, bands, and recording studio time. 'The guy was such a big spender from the beginning, even with the James band when he was getting paid chicken-feed wages', a musician says, 'that he ran out of money faster than it came in. And he began to feel that Dorsey was stealing most of it.'

Sinatra went to a lawyer instead of continuing to give Dorsey his cut. When the word got out and reporters asked Frank about it, he said, 'You can quote Sinatra as saying that he believes it is wrong for anybody to own a piece of him and collect on it when that owner is doing nothing for Sinatra.' Dorsey promptly asked a court to attach Sinatra's earnings for his failure to live up to a legal contract and pay his due, which is when Sinatra fans began picketing theatres where the Dorsey band was playing. Eventually, Sinatra got out of the Dorsey contract.

The official version of the deal was that Sinatra agreed to sign with Music Corporation of America as his talent agency. MCA paid Dorsey $35,000 and Sinatra paid him another $25,000, which he got from Columbia Records as an advance against royalties. At the same time, MCA agreed to split its earnings on Sinatra until 1948 with General Amusement Corporation, the organization Sinatra had originally signed with when he first left the Dorsey band. Whoever put the package together at MCA must have become a legend at the agency: Over the next ten years, its commissions on Sinatra totalled about six million dollars. Sinatra was exuberant about the settlement. 'I now own myself', he told reporters.

That's the official version of Sinatra's contract buy-back. The unofficial one, long a favourite tale where Mafia men get together and, though never provable, also a part of an extensive Justice Department file on Sinatra's Mafia connections, has it that one Willie Moretti, the Don in the area of New Jersey where Sinatra grew up and a friend of the Sinatra family, stepped in personally to settle the dispute with Dorsey. The band leader was adamant: He would not, for anything in the world, give up his nearly half-share of Sinatra's future earnings. Moretti was furious at Dorsey's unethical behaviour; the band leader, Moretti suggested, was a bigger racketeer than any mob man could ever be. One night Moretti showed up in Dorsey's dressing room, shoved a gun into the mouth that was more accustomed to a trombone, and suggested he sell Sinatra's contract. Dorsey sold. The price, the story goes, was precisely one dollar.

It doesn't take too much perception to realize that what is so often described as Sinatra's 'arrogance' is his emotional reaction to those many times in his past when he was deeply hurt by the Harry Cohns and other entertainment industry barons, and most particularly by the press. From the very beginning, when he was making the girls scream, faint, and masturbate in their seats, Frank was described by most writers as a skinny, untalented guy who had somehow discovered the perverted secret of how to mind-fuck pubescent women. Later, when that kind of brainless criticism stopped, mainly because musicians, jazz artists, and other singers, most notably Billie Holliday, began to state publicly that Frank was indeed a very *great* singer, his detractors shifted gears.

Sinatra worked for the reelection of Franklin Delano

Roosevelt in 1944; he punched out anyone who dared use the words 'nigger', 'kike', or 'dago' within his hearing; he very strenuously and vocally fought for the underdog, the minority groups which were being mistreated by the American power structure. And the writers of the Hearst newspapers, particularly, who always saw Communists under every bed, went after Sinatra with every innuendo they could get past their libel lawyers.

Sinatra fought back. Never offered equal time in the columns to reply to the accusations against him, Sinatra retaliated in the only manner available to a man with his background. He beat the hell out of Hearst columnist Lee Mortimer, his most vicious detractor. He attacked, from the stage, Dorothy Kilgallen, also employed by Hearst. And the ladies and gentlemen of the press, aghast at the temerity of the man in hitting back joined in to warn the public against this Public Enemy Number One named Francis Albert Sinatra.

Sinatra was 'arrogant' they said, because he made nasty cracks about Dorothy Kilgallen. But what the hell was so arrogant about criticizing somebody in a nightclub before only a few hundred people when she had been needling him in a column read by millions? Sinatra was disliked by a number of press photographers in New York who believed he ordered his driver to run down a persistent Hearst photographer. Other newspapermen say it never happened at all. The photographer's version is the one that's believed although Sinatra's is probably the truth.

After Sinatra had gathered a lot of unfavourable publicity because he had dared to hire a blacklisted Hollywood writer to do a screenplay for him, one columnist wrote: 'What's important is that he has gathered enemies because he does not bow and scrape whenever he sees a press card. The fact is that Sinatra is really hated because he is not a hypocrite. If a magazine publishes a story about him which he doesn't like, he says "Drop dead, creeps", and he refuses to help them with future stories. Now this is a shock to most members of the working press because we are accustomed to people smiling and lying to us even if they hate us, and an honest man is a dangerous thing. He could throw off our whole set of reflexes.'

The attitude of the press, in America and throughout the world, is that Sinatra owes it to journalists to bare his soul to them and to become public property because the press made him. That's a lot of nonsense. Frank excited the imagination of millions of people and the journalists rushed in to report the excitement because he was hot copy. When he was cold during those years that his voice left him and his fans stopped buying his records, he remained cold copy (except for the headlines over Ava) until he won the Oscar and the press again rushed to give its readers Sinatra stories.

All of which explains to some extent Sinatra's dumbest blunder – his battle with Australian journalists.

The entire affair started, say members of Sinatra's entourage, when a woman press agent working for the promoter of Frank's five-city, $650,000, Australian concert tour came to his Melbourne hotel room to discuss publicity. Frank's attitude must have been: 'What publicity? The joint is sold out and the papers have been printing reams of copy about me.' Still, the press agent began ticking off a long list of things that Sinatra *must* do, capped with the final order: 'You *must* hold a press conference.'

The one thing no person on earth ever gets away with is telling Sinatra what to do. You suggest, you beg, but you never order. If Frank thinks he's being pushed around, if he feels he's not being treated with the respect that is his due, he'll explode.

He exploded. He told the woman what to do with her press conference, using some choice expletives from the Hoboken docks. She rushed down to the lobby, where reporters and photographers were massed, and told them Sinatra refused to cooperate with the press. She also complained to the powerful journalists' union that she had been verbally abused.

The reporters rushed up to Sinatra's room, demanding to be seen. They were refused admittance. When it was time to go to Festival Hall to prepare for the concert, the burlier members of Frank's entourage, dubbed the 'goon squad' by the world's press, cleared a path for their leader. Reporters were shoved, some punches were thrown, and the battle that would get international headlines was joined.

Backstage at Festival Hall, Sinatra found another mob of journalists and photographers waiting to interview him. He became furious at their presence backstage, and well he should have, for in all theatre history nobody, not even the performer's wife or mother, is permitted backstage without specific permission of the performer, usually a written pass. Sinatra shoved his way past the newsmen. 'Get the hell out of my way!' he shouted.

Despite his anger, his singing was absolutely flawless. The audience of 6,200, who had paid a top price of $26 a ticket, gave him a standing ovation. The curtain went up again and Sinatra stepped out of the wings. Instead of doing an encore, as hoped and expected, Frank made a speech.

'Ladies and gentlemen', he said, 'I'm a little tired tonight. I had to run all day because of the parasites who chased us ... They won't quit; they wonder why I won't talk to them. I wouldn't drink water with them, let alone talk to them. Boy, oh boy, they're murder. They've got a name in the States for their counterparts. They call them parasites ... I say they're bums, and they're always going to be bums. ...

'It's the scandal men that bug you and drive you crazy, and the hookers – the broads of the press are the hookers of the press, need I explain this to you? I might offer a buck and a half, that's true. I once paid a broad in Washington two dollars, and I overpaid her. She didn't even bathe ... most of them don't anyway. ...'

(Sinatra's reference was to *Washington Post* columnist Maxine Cheshire. When it became public knowledge that Sinatra had become close to Agnew and had been boosting him for vice president, Cheshire's editors sent her to throw one question at Frank. 'Mr Sinatra', she asked as he stepped out of Ronald Reagan's limousine to attend some Republican function, 'do you think that your alleged association with the Mafia will prove to be the same embarrassment to Vice President Agnew as it was to the Kennedy administration?' Sinatra shrugged and said, 'I don't worry about things like that.' Cheshire was relieved. She had expected him to become angry and rude.

(But then Cheshire began repeating, on the cocktail circuit, the rumour that Barbara Marx was Agnew's girlfriend and Sinatra was simply camouflage for his friend. And on the second night of Nixon's inauguration celebration in January, 1973, Cheshire was reporting on a private party at Washington's Jockey Club when she approached Sinatra and Barbara Marx to chat with them. She was just introducing herself to Marx – whom she had interviewed by telephone several times – when Frank came over and absolutely exploded.

('Get away from me, you scum', he shouted at Cheshire. 'Go home and take a bath. I don't want to talk to you. I'm getting out of here to get rid of your stench. You know, Miss Cheshire, don't you, that stench you smell is coming from you?' His face reddening, Sinatra went on : 'You're nothing but a two-dollar cunt. C-U-N-T. You know what that means, don't you? You've been down for two dollars all your life.' He reached into his pocket, pulled out two one-dollar bills, and stuffed them into the glass that Cheshire was holding. 'Here, baby, that's what you're used to', he said. With that, he stalked off.)

Now, in Australia, he was giving the same opinion of Australian journalists. His rather insane speech continued for another few moments and then Sinatra finished up by shouting, 'We who have God-given talents say to hell with them!'

The audience, which had sat in silence, obviously stunned, now rose and began to boo and jeer Sinatra. He ran off-stage and was met by those same reporters he had just called whores. Once more his 'goon squad' helped him bull through their mass and he, Barbara Marx, Mickey Rudin, and the rest made it back to their suites at the Southern Cross Hotel. Another group of journalists were waiting in the corridor, and Sinatra's party again forced its way through. This time, a woman TV reporter and two cameramen were cut about the head and face.

The news of Sinatra's dreadful behaviour flashed over TV and was written in screaming headlines in every paper on the continent. And some powerful Australians decided to teach

Frankie a lesson. The next stop on his tour was Sydney. Frank was planning to fly out of Melbourne in the Gulfstream Mark II jet he owned, a plush plane with twelve seats, a bar, and a bedroom suite. But when he awoke the next afternoon he learned that his plane would never get off the ground. Robert Hawkes, head of the Australian Council of Labour Unions and a power in the Australian Labour Party, announced, 'I have ordered the maintenance men at the airport not to inject even a single ounce of jet fuel into Mr Sinatra's plane.' And Hawkes went on TV and said, 'Sinatra will never get out of the country until he apologizes.'

Sinatra was a prisoner in Melbourne. A hungry prisoner, it soon became apparent. For Hawkes's power reached into many other areas. The unionized hotel staff was ordered not to deliver anything up to Sinatra's room. When somebody up in the suit called to order food and drink, he was told. 'Sorry, sir. We are not permitted to serve you.'

Rudin, Sinatra's lawyer, immediately opened negotiations with the union leaders, but nothing much came of it. Someone went out to the airport to check the amount of fuel in the jet's tanks and learned there was just enough to fly to Sydney. So Sinatra and his party left (Sinatra lying across the seat in his limousine to avoid photographers) and continued to the next stop on the concert tour. On his arrival in Sydney, Frank learned that the stagehands' union had decided not to work at his concert.

Sinatra sent out word that he wanted the press to apologize to him, which got a lot of laughs. Then there were ultimatums from Hawkes and other labour leaders that he'd better apologize by the next morning, or else. That evening, Rudin met with the union leaders and a compromise was worked out. Obviously, everyone involved came to realize the entire battle was beginning to make everyone look stupid. Only a few journalists apologized, apparently to Frank's satisfaction. Sinatra completed his tour, keeping his mouth shut – except when he used it to 'humiliate' Barbara Marx – then went on to perform in Japan.

No other entertainer in the world would have escalated a press agent's over-enthusiasm into an international incident, one that even prompted Prince Charles to comment, in what he thought was an off-the-record interview, that Frank was 'a pretty strange person' who keeps 'creeps' and 'Mafia types' around him all the time.

A publicist who once worked for Sinatra said, 'Frank's been in business all his life and yet he'll never learn. Any other star would have had his press agent explain that Mr Sinatra doesn't hold press conferences, doesn't even give interviews. But, because Mr Sinatra simply *loves* the Australians, he'll make an exception to the rule. He'll consent to a pool interview – one reporter, one photographer, and they share it with all the newspapers.

'Then you make it clear to the reporter selected that he shouldn't ask Frank about his love life, or about the Mafia. Mr Sinatra is giving you a special treat, blah, blah, blah. And Frank can do the rest. He's charming. When he wants to he can charm anybody, and I mean anybody. Instead of exploding and calling them names, Frank should have just turned on the charm. I just don't think Frank will ever learn how to handle the press.'

But that's not completely true. Perhaps he's unable to deal with the ordinary hard-nosed journalist – the graduate of the police reporter school of journalism who's in the habit of being tough – but on a one-to-one basis he is capable of enormous graciousness. To cite but one example, a couple of years ago Sinatra did a benefit concert at Carnegie Hall in New York. Jan Hodenfield, pop music critic and columnist for the *New York Post*, published a review the next day which said, in effect, that although Sinatra's voice had lost some of its range, although he made a number of technical mistakes in his singing, Frank still possessed that magic ability to reach his audience and captivate them. On the whole, a fair but not adulatory review. A couple of days later, Hodenfield received a letter from Sinatra, thanking him for what he'd written.

CHAPTER 2

Studying his life and interviewing his friends as well as his enemies makes one thing about Frank Sinatra very clear : He has a compulsive need for power.

'Frank Sinatra relishes power', one man who knows him well has said. 'He enjoys the use of power more than any other public figure I can think of, except maybe Howard Hughes and former President Nixon. You see, I've always felt Frank still thinks of himself as an underdog, and building a power base was the one way to keep from being stepped on like all the other underdogs are.'

When Sinatra first went to Hollywood in 1943, he was the most popular entertainer in the country (even though he had yet to make his first film) and the entire tinsel-town rolled over and begged him to scratch its stomach. It was then that Frank got his first taste of the power of fame, and he used it to build up a retinue of important Hollywood figures whose lives revolved around the personal magnetism of its leader.

For the most part, they were people with whom Frank did business – or, to put it another way, people to whom Frank could throw business. Julie Styne and Sammy Cahn practically became Frank's personal songwriters, and in return they did the music for many of his early films. Another member of the set was Axel Stordahl; formerly with Dorsey, he became Frank's arranger and conductor. Gene Kelly, Skitch Henderson, Peter Lawford, Jo Davidson, the sculptor, Benson Ford and other members of the Ford family – Sinatra's friends spread across broad lines.

But those were simply the superficial friends, the ones who

ran around taking part in Frank's public capers. The other friends, those beholden to him for a variety of reasons, included many of the most powerful men in Hollywood. 'He ran a little Mafia out there', a former Hollywood producer recalls. 'He included in it all the best actors, the best producers, the best directors. They controlled everything and he controlled them. They adored him, and they were afraid of him. Sinatra made a lot of them. And they were afraid because they knew he could un-make them just as fast.'

Another figure from that era recalls, 'Sinatra was always making deals, and including people so they'd make money, too. He was one of the first to start his own song-publishing company, right from the beginning. He bought into restaurants, clubs, all sorts of businesses, and they all made money for him and for the friends he counted in. Frank was the guy who made things *happen*. He kept looking for more things to do because he had to keep busy. He had to work eighteen hours a day because work was more important than any of the broads out there he fucked – and he probably fucked them all – and because he's really a very lonely guy who can't stand being alone with the one person he's really afraid to face – Frank Sinatra.'

Sinatra won the loyalty of a large minority of the movie colony, not only because of his personal magnetism, but by his enormous generosity. To his friends, real or imagined, Sinatra gave hundreds of gold watches, cigarette lighters, cuff-links, tie-pins, and even Cadillacs. He gave friends jobs in his films. He went out with women simply to give them national publicity, for any starlet who dated Frank immediately got her photo into the papers and fan magazines. And he won the undying loyalty of those who counted most in Hollywood.

In a way, he seemed to be emulating his mother, a Hoboken politician who had been able to guarantee the local Democratic Party machine about five hundred votes each election by helping the people in her district. As one of Sinatra's friends expressed it back then, 'When he isn't being the most open-handed guy in the world, both his fists are clenched. That's the way they play politics in Hudson

County, New Jersey, and I suppose that's where he learned it – from his mother, Dolly.' Mrs Sinatra was a ward heeler for the Hague Democratic machine in the old days. She was the local politician who doled out the sacks of coal and the baskets of food in her district. She knew everybody by their first names, and whenever anyone got into any trouble, she was always the first one to come around to help. Her door was always open and she used to encourage people to knock on it twenty-four hours a day. That's the way you win friends and influence votes. And that's what her son, Frankie, was doing in Hollywood. Eventually, he would try to turn his own special brand of vote-getting into political influence.

Sinatra's first brush with national political power came almost by accident one afternoon in September, 1944, less than two months before election day. Frank and a group of his boys were having drinks in Toots Shor's restaurant in Manhattan when Shor was called away to the phone. When he returned to the table he announced grandly, 'I just got a call from the White House. They want me and my wife to come down for a reception for FDR. My wife can't go because she's sick, so I told them I'm bringing along Frank Sinatra and Rags Ragland.'

A few days later the singer, the comedian, and the restaurateur were in the White House having tea with President Roosevelt. When he emerged some time later, Sinatra told the waiting reporters, I feel as if I've seen a vision. . . .' He was so magnetized by Roosevelt that he promptly decided to campaign for Roosevelt's fourth term. All of Frank's advisers were against his getting involved in politics except for George Evans, his press agent. Evans felt that it was time for Sinatra to reach out to an older audience – the bobby-soxers still remained almost his only fans – and taking part in a political campaign could help make Frank appealing to those older adults who adored Roosevelt.

Sinatra began to make speeches for Roosevelt – 'He's the kind of man you'd want for your father', Frank often said – and he contributed thousands of dollars to the Democratic campaign treasury. 'Of course, he's a Democrat', said his mother, the long-term party worker. 'What else is there?'

As Sinatra himself would later write: 'My first real criticism from the press came when I campaigned for President Roosevelt in 1944. A few columnists took me to task, insisting that entertainers should stick to entertaining...Ginger Rogers, George Murphy, and other stars supported Tom Dewey during this campaign, and I noted that none of my critics lambasted *them*.'

Of course not, because they supported the Republican candidate. For the first time, Sinatra began to develop a dislike for a certain kind of newspaperman – the right-wing bigot who will cheer John Wayne because he's politically conservative, but who will attack Frank Sinatra because he was a liberal Democrat. Westbrook Pegler, Lee Mortimer, and many other anti-Roosevelt writers who worked for the Hearst and Scripps-Howard supermarket journalism chains grew apoplectic because Frank dared express a choice of candidate. Sinatra knew perfectly well that had he supported the Republican candidate, the Peglers of the profession, the propagandists posing as journalists, would have cheered him on.

Sinatra supported Harry Truman and Adlai Stevenson and local Democrats in later election years, but it wasn't until John F. Kennedy's campaign in 1960 that he actually seemed to be reaching for real political power on a national level. Before that, however, came his fall.

It is possible to trace Sinatra's enormous need to be influential, in the sixties and into this decade, to the ego-bruising, humiliating destruction of his career during the several years before he rose again after winning the Academy Award.

It must be remembered that after a couple of years of going slowly downhill, Sinatra's career all but ended in 1952. His records did not sell at all. He played the New York Paramount, the scene of his earliest triumphs, and the balcony was empty. In a Chicago nightclub that seats 1,200, only 150 fans showed up. CBS had signed Sinatra to do a TV series, but they tore up the contract after the ratings and the notices proved disappointing. The network had been unable to find more than a single sponsor to buy time on the show. Finally, MCA dropped him – even though Frank had earned the agency $693,000 in commissions the previous year. It was, a Sinatra friend said, 'the final indignity, the kiss-off of a fallen idol'.

'The hurt was deep and lasting.' Sinatra admitted. 'Can you imagine being fired by an agency that never had to sell you?'

Then came the little gold-plated Oscar, with which he once again made himself a man of power in Hollywood, in national entertainment circles, and in certain political areas. Although Sinatra won it for a supporting rather than a starring role, his Oscar represented a comeback story that captured not only the imagination of Hollywood, but also of the world. The award for his sensitive portrayal in *Eternity* proved that, in addition to the voice which had made him a star, Sinatra had the ability to act. Producers, directors, and studio bosses came begging him to star in *their* films. He demanded, and got, $250,000 for each film he accepted.

There can be little doubt that, once he shot back to the top clutching his Oscar, the hurts that he felt only the year before, when MCA dropped him, crystallized into a single overwhelming need to attain such enormous wealth and influence that he would always be able to control his own artistic and financial destiny. Starting in 1953, the man who had always thought of himself as an underdog began working at a desperate pace to gain the status and amass the riches that all the other powerful Establishment figures possess.

In 1952 Sinatra's income had consisted mostly of what he could borrow from friends and what Ava Gardner gave him. Within a few years, he had large interests in real estate, record companies, music publishing firms, prize fighters, hotels, restaurants, and 9 percent ownership of the Sands, the Las Vegas gambling den. After making a few films for others, on a straight quarter-million-dollar salary for each, Sinatra formed Essex Productions and began to demand, as part of the fee for his services, a share in the ownership of his films. Essex produced the Capitol Records sound track of *High Society*. Essex owned 25 percent of *Pal Joey*, and another Sinatra company owned the same percentage of *The Joker is Wild*. Frank had also made a deal whereby Essex

Productions owned all the masters of the recordings he made and simply 'leased' them to his new record distributor, Capitol. In almost everything in which Sinatra became involved, he was the businessman partner at the same time that he was the artist. He was becoming Sinatra, Inc., with interests far afield of the entertainment business as well – Sinatra now owns his own airline, a missile parts company, and real estate interests across the country, with a personal staff of close to one hundred men to run it all for him.

In 1960, Frank took the enormous step of putting together his own record company, Reprise Records, with financial backing from Warner Brothers. One day late that year, while strolling past the newly built Capitol Tower on Vine Street with Morris Ostin, an executive of Reprise, Frank stopped and looked up at the skeleton of the building and said, 'I helped build that. Now let's build one of my own.' Through most of 1961, the first actual year of production for Reprise, Frank devoted much of his time to his company's business. He made and released three of his own albums on the Reprise label, plus two films, but his greatest energies went into watching over his $25 million worth of investment. (He sold Reprise to Warner Brothers in 1962, for a $27 million capital gain and continued control over his own recordings.)

'When I think of myself five years hence (when he would be 50), I see myself not so much as an entertainer as a high-level executive, interested in business, perhaps in directing and producing films', he told writer Joe Hyams in one of his rare interviews. 'The things I'm involved in personally, such as acting and recording, steadily earn less money, while the things I have going for me earn the most. And that's the way I want it to be.'

A year later he told Robin Douglas-Home, 'I've been performing out front for nearly thirty years now and frankly I'm getting a bit tired. Now I want to do more and more behind the scenes, using my head. Finance fascinates me.'

At the same time that he was moving heavily into the business end of entertainment, Sinatra refined and extended the control he had wielded over a large part of Hollywood in the Forties. The so-called Rat Pack and later the Clan – which were generally pictured as a group of hard-drinking, hard-playing anti-Establishment figures – were in actuality *Il Padrone*'s 'family', the 'little Mafia' of the old days now become Sinatra's army. They not only played together, but they worked together – for Sinatra's benefit and their own. Dean Martin, for example, left his record company and went to Reprise. He also got roles in a number of Sinatra films. Sinatra usually chooses his co-stars from among his drinking buddies, and he hands out other parts in his films with the same generosity with which he passes out $200 gold cigarette lighters. Richard Breen, the screenwriter on Sinatra's 1960 film, *Oceans 11*, told a writer that Sinatra kept telephoning with requests that he write in new parts for new friends. 'Mr Sinatra is a genial man around the restaurants', Breen said. 'He has a tendency to drop by a table and say hello to someone and before he finishes that someone is in the picture.'

One Hollywood columnist tried to explain why Sinatra and his Clan seemed to play such a large role in the town's social and business affairs. 'There's nothing worse in this town than being in the out-group', he said. 'There's a whole new era out here. All the people who used to sneer at Frank's group now want to be in it, and if they don't want to be in it, they at least are intrigued or interested by it.

'In the old days the ultra, ultra group would have nothing to do with this jazzy crowd. Now they all covet it. Like Peter Lawford, who used to play it so grand, or the producer, Bill Goetz – I mean the type of people who own real Matisses, real Van Goghs, the type of people who not only live gracefully but who run this town.

'The result has been a whole new social group and a whole new set of professional and social standards. There's a whole new era in Hollywood and it's all motivated by a skinny little kid from Hoboken.'

Some writers claimed, back in those days, that Sinatra's 'enormous power' was a menace to the entertainment business. An article in *Good Housekeeping* magazine, for example, warned the American public that Frank was 'a law unto himself' and had become 'the most feared man in Hollywood.'

It concluded with this ominous appraisal of Sinatra's influence: 'It would be disturbing indeed if this enormous power were in the hands of a completely stable and predictable human being. When it is in the hands of a man torn by emotions that he apparently either cannot or does not care to control, it is something to view with alarm.'

Certainly, Sinatra the businessman and Godfather of sorts had then, and still has, a large amount of influence over the entertainment industry. But if he possessed even a fraction of the power attributed to him, he would probably have held back the rise of the Beatles, the Rolling Stones, and all the other younger artists whose records outsold his in the Sixties and whose music he admittedly did not understand or even like; had he the power some claimed he possessed, he would never have been forced to sell his holdings in Nevada gambling casinos because of his associations with a major Chicago *mafioso*; had he such power, he would never have been forced to compromise his noted defence of the underdog and capitulate to the conservative press by firing a blacklisted Communist screenwriter after publicly stating he thought it was time to make up for what had been done to such men, the members of the Hollywood Ten.

In fact, Alfred G. Aronowitz, a reporter with whom I worked on the series of articles on Sinatra for our newspaper, spent many weeks in Hollywood trying to sniff out evidence of Sinatra's inordinate power. The best he could come up with was an anecdote supplied by an actress named Gloria Rhoads, who had dated Sinatra occasionally. Miss Rhoads apparently made the mistake of writing the biography of another woman who had dated Sinatra more steadily. The book, Miss Rhoads said, was written so that it wouldn't embarrass Sinatra, but when she brought it to *them* – apparently Sinatra lawyers or advisers – for Frank's approval, one of them told her, 'If you pursue this you will never work another day in Hollywood. We are very powerful and we don't hesitate to use this power. We can call up any top studio and tell them not to use you and they will not.' From that point on, Miss Rhoads told Aronowitz, she couldn't get another movie job.

Comments a Hollywood producer not known for his love of Sinatra, 'The whole thing's a joke. Sure, Frank could have blacklisted any crummy starlet; almost any star can do that in this town 'cause there's a million so-called starlets around. What does it mean? Could he have stopped anybody from using Marilyn Monroe? Or any *importamt* actor? Like Brando. Frank hates Brando, really hates him. Would anybody in this town listen if Frank called and said, "Don't use Brando?" No way. Yeah, Frank has a tight circle of buddies and they run around rooting for each other. Sure, he can make a star out of Juliet Prowse or anyone he wants to promote. But he can't break anybody really important. Not even Howard Hughes can do that in this town.'

What it really comes down to is that many writers, and the Hollywood types who feed them their material, are publicly horrified because Sinatra demands and gets an enormous amount of loyalty from the people within his circle; when he doesn't get it, when he feels he's been slighted or imagines he's been doublecrossed, then he often behaves like a boor. Or a *gaffone*, as his father would have said, a peasant without class, which is strange in a man whose entire image is built on absolute class.

'Frank demands 200 percent loyalty', a songwriter who was a member of the Clan at that time has said. 'One hundred per cent with him and 100 per cent with him with anybody else. For instance, when you're with him you can't be a friend of anybody who's not with him. Suppose I might tell him I got a deal running with Mitch Miller. You know, Frank blames Miller for trying to ruin his career. Well, suppose I had a chance to go in and make some money in something that involves Miller. Frank would say to me, "What do you want to have anything to do with him for? Get away from me, you creep!"'

Back then, when he was increasing his power base, and even today, when he has probably reached the apex of his power, give or take a few million and a company or two, Sinatra's friends always knew precisely how Frank felt about something or someone – they had only to *look* at him.

For example – and although it's almost a twenty-year-old

example, it is still the most revealing one available – when Frank was filming *Guys and Dolls* he was both jealous and angry at Marlon Brando because he was given the part Sinatra wanted, the lead role of Sky Masterson, even though Brando couldn't carry a tune and had to take vocal instructions. (Sinatra still appears to loathe Brando, which is perhaps why Sinatra suggested to Francis Ford Coppola that they buy the film rights to *The Godfather* and he'd play the title role.) Frank's anger at Brando, say those who were around at the time, stemmed not only from the fact that Sinatra had lost the opportunity to sing the major love ballads in the film, but also because it deprived him of the chance to make royalties on the songs by capitalizing on them as a recording artist.

His anger intensified when filming began. Sinatra is a spontaneous performer, or so he believes; he often refuses to do more than one or two takes of any scene because he feels his strength as an actor is his spontaneity and if he is forced to repeat a scene too often he becomes wooden. (As an aside, several directors who have worked with Frank, including Billie Wilder, have said that if he worked at his acting and took it seriously, he would be one of the finest actors in the world.) Because he bores easily, he'd rather be elsewhere once he's done a scene, and he rationalizes his short attention span as 'spontaneity'. In any case, Brando's method acting required constant rehearsal and polish, and a dozen or more retakes of every major scene. After a while, Frank wouldn't even talk to Brando.

'So nobody from Frank's entourage would talk to anybody from Brando's entourage', says an actress who worked in the film. 'When Brando tried to make friends with Frank, he also told the guys in his entourage to try to make friends with the guys in Frank's entourage. Brando kept holding strategy conferences with his entourage in his dressing room, until they finally gave up trying. But Frank didn't have to call any conferences. His group just knew what to do.'

A question no one has ever been able to answer is why adult men and women will follow their leader in such adolescent behaviour; why they often seem to promote in Frank the need to punch out columnists, parking lot attendants, and heckling nightclub patrons. For that matter, why Frank himself sometimes provokes public scenes and confrontations. I don't mean the occasions when he is personally provoked into violence – and that has happened more often than appears on the surface, despite newspaper accounts – but those times when Frank himself boorishly starts it all apparently for the sheer joy of it.

One night some years ago Sinatra was in a private club in Beverly Hills, a club in which he is the most famous and influential member. Standing at the bar, he seemed tired and withdrawn, as if he were a man alone in the world. Members of his circle explained to friends that Frank had a cold.

After a while Sinatra left the bar and walked toward a small billiard room behind the bar where Leo Durocher, one of Frank's closest friends, was shooting pool. The moment Frank stepped out of his self-imposed isolation and left the bar, a number of men in the club began to move. Brad Dexter, a big and strong actor considered Frank's bodyguard, left the table at which he was sitting with friends – his eyes had been constantly darting toward the bar where *Il Padrone* sat – and followed Sinatra into the pool room. Although an actor with several film and TV credits, Dexter is best known in Beverly Hills because he saved Sinatra from drowning off a beach in Hawaii a couple of years earlier. Frank rewarded him by making him a producer in his film company, giving him a posh office near Sinatra's own, and keeping him close by almost as a good luck charm. Dexter's role, whether on assignment from Frank or one he assumed for himself, was to step in before someone could provoke the boss into throwing a punch and generating more ugly headlines about his hot temper and his God-like attitude. It is Dexter, incidentally, who once said of Sinatra, 'I'd kill for him.'

When Sinatra walked into the pool room, followed by Dexter, he seemed to scowl slightly at the young men hanging around watching the billiard game, men dressed in *mod* clothing: velour shirts, velvet slacks, and Italian loafers. Sinatra's style, that evening and at all times except the most casual, was immaculately conservative – an oxford-grey suit with a waistcoat, a quietly-patterned tie, shoes that appeared to have been polished only seconds before. Sinatra seemed most intrigued by a pair of sixty-dollar Game Warden boots. He looked at the boots, turned to look at the billiard table, looked again at the boots. His eyes became riveted on them, so much so that he didn't seem to notice the man in them, Harlan Ellison, a writer who had recently completed the script of *The Oscar*.

Finally, Sinatra could no longer remain silent. 'Hey', he shouted in a voice made harsh by his sore throat. 'Those Italian boots?'

'No', Ellison said.

'Spanish?'

'No.'

'Are they *English* boots?'

Ellison frowned. 'Look, I dunno, man', he said, then turned away.

Durocher, about to shoot, froze over his stick. The room fell silent. Frank Sinatra had *punched* men with less provocation. Sinatra walked over to Ellison, the room absolutely silent except for the sound of Sinatra's steps, and said, 'You expecting a *storm*?'

'Look', Ellison shot back, 'is there any reason why you're talking to me?'

'I don't like the way you're dressed', Sinatra said. His blue eyes, now cold and hard, swept over Ellison's clothing, a green wool sweater, brown corduroy slacks, and tan suede jacket.

'Hate to shake you up', Ellison said, 'but I dress to suit myself.'

Someone in Ellison's group suggested they leave, but he refused. Sinatra asked what Ellison did for a living and he replied, 'I'm a plumber.' One of the young men in the room shouted that he was a writer and had just finished the screenplay of *The Oscar*. Sinatra said, 'I've seen it and it's a piece of crap.'

'That's strange', Ellison said. 'They haven't even released it yet.'

Sinatra repeated, 'I've seen it, and it's a piece of crap.'

After a few more exchanges, Ellison left the room. Later, Sinatra found the assistant manager of the club and barked, 'I don't want anybody in here without coats and ties.' The man nodded, and the rule was subsequently passed. (The manager, having received word that Sinatra was involved in another scene, had fled the club and driven home for the night.)

Years later a former Sinatra employee who was there that night said of the incident, 'Frank was bored when he picked on Ellison. He wasn't very serious about any of it, just a bit of a game to break the boredom and forget his troubles. His marriage to Mia was going bad, he was afraid CBS was going to mention Mafia in a TV show they were doing on his life, a lot of things were off that night. And he had a cold. When Frank has a cold, a major part of Hollywood trembles.'

In 1960, for the first time in all his years of political campaigning, Frank Sinatra began to realize it was possible to compound his business investments through political contacts at the very top – the White House.

'He actually preferred Hubert Humphrey as the Democratic candidate in 1960 because Humphrey was an old friend he thought he could have some influence with', says a former speechwriter for John F. Kennedy. 'But when it became obvious that Jack Kennedy was going to get the nomination, he jumped aboard. After all, Peter Lawford was married to Kennedy's sister, Pat, and Lawford was a member of the Clan. So it all fell into place for Frank. His boy was going to be President.'

But long before the Democratic convention which chose Kennedy, Sinatra learned that he would have to compromise his principles – something he had never done before – if he was going to gather any kind of political influence. Very quietly in early 1960, Frank had hired Albert Maltz to write the screenplay for *The Execution of Private Slovick*, a book about the only American soldier executed by the U.S. Army since the Civil War. Maltz had not received a screen credit since his conviction in June, 1950, for contempt of Congress for refusing to compromise *his* principles by naming other Hollywood figures who had been members of the Communist party. Maltz spent almost a year in prison and could not find work in Hollywood when he was released (although he, Dalton Trumbo, and others of the Hollywood Ten had sold screenplays under pseudonyms and at much lower fees than they would normally have commanded).

'Sinatra decided this was all hypocrisy', a friend said later. 'The studios were using Maltz, Trumbo, and other guys and cheating them out of the going rates for top writing talent. Frank said, "Screw it, these guys were victims of a witch hunt and now they're being robbed by the studios. I'm going to get it into the open." '

Sinatra knew, however, that a public announcement of Maltz's writing assignment would provoke an outcry from the Hearst press, the John Birch Society, and other organizations that were still blaming the Democratic Woodrow Wilson for permitting the Russian Revolution to take place and the Democratic Franklin Roosevelt for selling out at Yalta. He knew, too, that the right-wing fanatics would use Maltz as ammunition against John Kennedy. To prevent possible harm to Kennedy's chances at the nominating convention, Sinatra kept the Maltz project a secret.

But on 21st March the *New York Times* broke the story, and the news provoked the expected storm. The Hearst press attacked Sinatra, suggesting Kennedy would bear the burden of the responsibility; veterans' groups said they would boycott and picket the film; other groups made threats of their own; in Hollywood, John Wayne publicly berated Sinatra for his act.

After eighteen days of controversy, Frank Sinatra backed down and announced, in a statement to reporters and in newspaper ads, that because of 'the reactions of my family, my friends, and the American public', he was making a settlement with Maltz and taking the writing assignment away from him.

Sinatra later said he dropped Maltz because he could

never have made the film with him as the screenwriter; the banks wouldn't give him the necessary financing. Yet, at the height of the attacks on Sinatra, Otto Preminger revealed he had hired Dalton Trumbo to do the screenplay for *Exodus*, and Stanley Kramer had hired still a third blacklisted writer, Nedrich Young, for *Inherit the Wind*. Both Preminger and Kramer refused to back down, although they also were sharply attacked. In truth, there was another reason for Sinatra's change of heart.

A former Kennedy aide says, 'The old man just put his foot down. Joe Kennedy called Sinatra and told him he'd either have to drop Maltz or disassociate himself from Jack Kennedy's campaign. Sinatra dropped Maltz. A friend in the White House was more important to him at the time than any fight over principle.'

Around the time of the Maltz imbroglio, the Kennedy family was preparing for the primary elections in Wisconsin, dumping millions of dollars in the state to help John Kennedy beat Humphrey and hopefully overwhelm all opposition. Bobby Kennedy informed Sinatra that he was being 'dismissed' as a Kennedy campaigner, not only because of the Maltz affair but because, as Peter Lawford later explained, 'Senator Humphrey's boys had passed out pamphlets saying Jack's glamorous friends from Hollywood were coming to bedazzle the voters. Jack's advisers thought it might cause hard feelings, so we didn't go into the state.' Lawford, Kennedy's brother-in-law, was himself told to stay away, as was Sammy Davis. Nevertheless, though Sinatra and his Clan stayed away, the Leader's voice boomed out of Kennedy sound trucks all over the state, singing the Kennedy campaign song, 'High Hopes', written by Sammy Cahn and Jimmy Van Heusen, two other members of the Sinatra circle.

The convention was held that July in Los Angeles. Father Joe Kennedy was hiding out in the Beverly Hills home of former film star and Hearst mistress Marion Davies, making himself felt behind the scenes at the convention, but staying away to avoid the charge that his wealth was buying the nomination for his son. The elder Kennedy did make the scene at one party, however, showing up at Sinatra's posh pad in Beverly Hills and getting slightly drunk.

Sinatra threw himself completely into the campaign, raising funds for Kennedy, involving all his friends. At the convention, Frank was very much in evidence on the floor (the back of his head painted black to prevent the TV cameras from picking up the high gloss of his bald pate), running errands for the Kennedys, talking to delegates still on the fence in an attempt to charm them into voting for Jack, politicking as his mother must have done back in New Jersey. When Kennedy was nominated, Sinatra redoubled his activities, taking part in both fund-raising and vote-getting meetings.

But the Kennedy advisers – primarily Bobby Kennedy, it was reported – were concerned over what the swinging Sinatra might do to the attempts to change John Kennedy's image from that of a playful young Senator to that of a mature statesman. After conferring with his older brother, Bobby notified Sinatra to keep a low campaign profile. 'He practically told Frank to get lost', says the former Kennedy aide. 'The thing that finally did it is when word leaked out in some column or other that Sinatra and the Clan privately referred to Jack Kennedy as "Jack the Ripper". That did it, as far as Bobby was concerned. But in spite of the fact that Sinatra was considered a political liability, he raised a lot of money for Jack's campaign, and he got a lot of people in Hollywood to forget their fears of getting involved in politics and come out and fight for Kennedy. And Jack appreciated that. He felt very warmly toward Frank, and Frank could have written his own ticket at the White House.'

'The joke going around', says another Kennedy aide, 'was that Frank wanted to be named ambassador to the Vatican, this guy who was the biggest swordsman in the world and twice divorced. Still, it wasn't a joke. There was always the feeling among the Kennedy people that Sinatra would have loved a government post, an ambassadorship or something of the sort. It would have been the capstone to his career, the kid from the docks who made it to the top. I mean, he even started to change his image for Kennedy, publicly disassociating himself from the Clan, trying to come across more respectable, even changing his tailor from some flash Hollywood guy to Cary Grant's tailor.

'It might have worked. The thing few people seem to understand is that Jack Kennedy was a star-fucker. Would you believe it? Here's the guy, the President of the United States, young rich and handsome, a superstar in his own right, and he was enamoured of the Hollywood glamour. And glamorous Hollywood women. He got a bigger kick out of meeting a famous star than he did from meeting Khruschev or de Gaulle. Marilyn Monroe singing at Jack's birthday party in Madison Square Garden, that was a highlight for him. And Sinatra is the man who convinced Marilyn to do it. Sinatra supplied a need for Jack Kennedy. He could have gotten a lot from the White House if it hadn't been for that Mafia stuff.'

After Robert Kennedy became Attorney General, he asked the FBI to make a study of Sinatra's relationship with important members of the American Mafia. 'All Bobby wanted to know was whether the administration could be embarrassed by Sinatra's associates', one of the former Kennedy aides told me. 'The answer he got back was yes, and it was accompanied by a full dossier on Sinatra.'

Because of that report and because of an incident involving a Chicago Mafia man (see chapter 4), John Kennedy dropped Frank from his circle of friends, publicly. The President had been scheduled to visit Palm Springs and had planned to stay at Sinatra's guest house. Sinatra had, in fact, added a presidential wing to his desert mansion solely to accommodate Kennedy and his family. (He called it the Kennedy Wing then; later, it became the Agnew Wing.) But after Bobby Kennedy warned his brother about Sinatra's Mafia friendships, the President stayed at Bing Crosby's house instead.

But that was only for public consumption. Former Kennedy aides have said that Bobby was the prime mover in an attempt to cut Sinatra off from the President; Bobby had several motives, it is said by those who worked with him, not the least of which was the fear that Sinatra, possessed of enormous charm and a magnetic personality, might gain so much influence over the President that Younger Brother's own influence would be eroded. President Kennedy, however, did not completely follow Bobby's advice to drop Sinatra cold, for Frank represented Hollywood and glamour and filled a special need for the President; privately, they maintained a friendly relationship.

That, however, was not enough to fill Sinatra's needs, for he is a man to whom the appearances of power are almost as important as the power itself. Naturally, Frank didn't care much for Bobby Kennedy. When Bobby announced he would seek the Democratic nomination for president in 1968, running against Sinatra's old friend and first choice as candidate in the 1960 election, Vice President Humphrey, Sinatra rushed to support Humphrey. But his attempts to help place a friend in the White House were short-circuited when his friendships with known Mafia leaders became a campaign issue and Humphrey politely asked him to drop out of the campaign.

Frank soon gave up on Democrats, who seemed to have a puritanical habit of checking up on his friends. He switched to the Republicans, who didn't seem to care at all about past rumours and scandals. Sinatra supported Ronald Reagan for governor of California in 1970 and made several appearances for Reagan's campaign. Reagan won.

He introduced Sinatra to Vice President Agnew, and they became close friends. Sinatra was a solid Republican now and was accepted by President Nixon even though Sinatra had supported Humphrey against Nixon two years before. Frank entertained at the White House in April, 1973, in the midst of his well-publicized retirement. Nixon suggested that Frank should come out of retirement and Sinatra replied, 'I'll consider that, Mr President.'

Precisely what benefits Sinatra gained from his role as a Republican insider, friend of the Vice President, and at least casual acquaintance of the President, may never be learned. Frank's name never came up in all the scandals surrounding Watergate – Howard Hughes's secret payment to Nixon people and the veritable sale of the White House to anyone with a few hundred thousand to spare – and there has never been a hint of any financial gain to Sinatra because of whatever influence he may have had over the two White House resident criminals. Perhaps simply sitting beside the great was benefit enough for Frank.

And it appears at this writing, that Sinatra will again take part in national politics. 'He'll probably start working for the Democrats pretty soon', a Sinatra associate said. 'But more quietly this time. He's not going to give anybody a chance to dump on him again by hitting him with that Mafia bullshit. He'll work behind the scenes.'

Another friend, however, claims Sinatra will support a Republican. No matter who gets Frank's support, one thing is certain – he'll also get Sinatra's complete loyalty. 'Frank's got a thing about loyalty', a Hollywood columnist says. 'He expects it from you, and he'll give it in return. Look at how loyal he's been to Agnew. Frank ended his retirement shortly after Agnew was forced to resign. A lot of us out here believe we know why. Because Frank had put so much into his friendship with Agnew that he had to prove his friend's disgrace wasn't the end of the Sinatra power. So he ended his retirement.'

He also demonstrated his loyalty in more tangible ways. After Agnew resigned and was set free by the court, Sinatra invited him to stay at his home in Palm Springs – still ostentatiously called the Agnew Wing – to recover from the shock of his disgrace. Sinatra threw parties for him, almost royal commands to the other Palm Springs social leaders that they must support Agnew in his hour of need. And it was Frank Sinatra who tried to persuade a New York publishing house to give the deposed Vice President an enormous advance for the novel he's writing.

Unfortunately, no journalist has ever gotten Dolly Sinatra's reaction to her son's concern for a man who disgraced the vice presidency, a man who bears the added cross of being a Republican.

Perhaps Ava Gardner, the one woman he seemed to have really loved deeply, thought she was cutting through some of the complexities of Sinatra's personality when she told an interviewer : 'Frank was a sacred monster. He was convinced there was nobody in the world except him.'

That's undoubtedly an oversimplication from a woman who still felt a lot of anger over the destruction of her marriage. A slight variation in her statement would have been a little closer to the truth : He was convinced there was nobody in the world except him and the people who are totally dependent on him. This is the concept of *Il Padrone* at its most refined, as Sinatra has refined it. He will drop everything to come to the aid of a man or woman who needs help, but the moment he feels the recipient of his largesse no longer truly depends upon him, Frank will cut off the relationship. The stories about his good deeds are almost legendary in Hollywood (and Sinatra has done nothing to promote them as legend; he has in fact, tried to keep most of them secret). But the stories about his sudden turnabout after the object of his good deed has been brought back to normal are also a part of the Sinatra legend.

In an interview some years ago, Lee J. Cobb remembered that when he had a heart attack it was Sinatra who rushed to his aid. 'We had made one movie together, but he was practically a stranger to me', Cobb recalled. Almost broke, hospitalized and afraid of dying, Cobb didn't know how he was going to pay his hospital bills. Suddenly Frank flashed into his life, bringing to the hospital room his own exuberance, the message not to worry about anything until you get better, and flowers, books, and a group of friends to cheer Cobb up. When Cobb had recovered sufficiently to leave the hospital, Frank flew him to Palm Springs as a house guest. Eventually the desert grew too hot for Cobb, so Frank moved him into a Hollywood apartment. And he paid whatever bills Cobb couldn't handle.

Later, Cobb said, 'After I recovered, our relationship tapered off until I hardly saw him at all. He seemed to disappear as soon as my need of him was over.'

But Sinatra can be brutal when he's decided a friend's need has ended and the friend is no longer a friend. 'Although Frank may need you', says a former friend, 'he wants to feel you need *him*. Once he feels you don't need him any more, then he picks a fight with you and you're finished.'

That's precisely what happened to Jule Styne, who once wrote music with Sammy Cahn exclusively for Sinatra. When Sinatra was down in the depths about losing Ava Gardner, Styne was deeply depressed over a broken romance. In spite of his own problems, Sinatra forced Styne to move into his apartment so he could help pull Styne back together again. For almost a year, Styne lived with Sinatra. Then, suddenly, he was asked to leave 'in no uncertain terms', as Styne later put it.

The reason Sinatra gave was that Styne had taken one of his best-selling songs to another firm for publication. That was obviously not the real reason, for the song had been published more than a year before; Frank had never said a word about it until he suddenly grew angry. The real reason, Styne is certain, is that he had begun to talk about leaving Hollywood and trying to write music for Broadway, meaning he was thinking of leaving Sinatra's sphere of influence. And Frank was hurt.

'You see', Styne told friends, 'I wanted to come to New York and get into the theatre. But Frank likes people to be dependent on him. And I wanted to feel that I could be independent of Frank, not spiritually, but financially. I wanted my own esteem.'

So Frank 'picked a fight' and Styne was ordered out. There is a line in Puzo's novel *The Godfather*, in which Don Corleone tells Johnny Fontane (the character Sinatra and everybody else in the world believes was loosely modelled on Frank): 'Friendship is everything. Friendship is more than talent. It is more than government. It is almost the equal of family. Never forget that.'

Sinatra must have learned that bromide as a child, for he has never forgotten it and he won't remain friends with anyone who does forget it. It is in that authentically Sicilian, and not necessarily Mafia, remark by the Godfather, and in Sinatra's childhood in an Italian ghetto, that the beginning of Frank as *Il Padrone* undoubtedly took shape.

*   *   *

'The house Frank was born in was on Monroe Street, a pretty good lower-middle-class neighbourhood. Definitely not slums', Sinatra's uncle, Dominick Garaventi, recalled during an interview years ago. But they were cold-water flats, another Hoboken resident and a friend of the family told me. No heat, no hot water, a toilet out in the hall on each floor, two families to a floor. The houses were fairly new tenements, perhaps ten years old, with none of the conveniences; typical turn-of-the-century, immigrant housing that would later decay into slums.

When he was born in that house on 12th December 1915, Frank weighed a little over thirteen pounds. The physician hampered by the baby's size, almost severed his ear and did lacerate his head pretty badly, leaving facial scars which Sinatra carries to this day. Mrs Josephine Monaco, one of Sinatra's aunts, who was present at the delivery, recalled later: 'The doctor said, "I don't think he'll live, so let's take care of the mother first." A few minutes later he attended to the baby, and to everyone's surprise the baby lived. He was a fat, healthy baby, too. Everyone jokes that he's been losing weight ever since he was born. But it wasn't until he was four or five that he got to be real skinny.'

The city in which he was born is a mile-square area of factories, railroads, and tenement-crowded streets; only its seedy waterfront offers a view of the Hudson River. At that time there was one bar for every 200 residents and, after 1920 one speakeasy for every 100 residents. Dominated by political corruption, Hoboken became the drinking and gambling resort for a wide area of New Jersey during Prohibition; its docks became one of several protected entry points for liquor from Canada, the West Indies, and Scotland.

Frank's mother – who was named Natalie because she was born on Christmas day, but who was always called Dolly – became the district leader for the Democratic party (the only party in town for all practical purposes) some time before the beginning of Prohibition. Politics seemed to come naturally to her. The daughter of a Sicilian grocer, she was a self-trained practical nurse but spent much of her time as a part-time barmaid in her husband's tavern. In those days, the taverns – and the speakeasies they became – were the centre of district-level political activity. Dolly fell into politicking quite naturally and with a distinctive flair.

'They called her Lady Bountiful', a neighbour remembered. 'People would run to her when they were in trouble or needed a favour and she would take them by the hand to City Hall. She was a beautiful woman, with strawberry blond hair, and people really loved her because she was good and she was generous. She would give out the Thanksgiving baskets for the really poor families and the Christmas clothes and bags of coal so they wouldn't freeze. And she would take them by the hand to vote on Election Day. Her district was always 100 per cent solid for the party.'

Mrs Rose Carrier, who lived most of her life opposite the house in which Frank was born and who became his babysitter when Frank was around three and his mother was working, remembers that 'Dolly started in politics when Frank was about five, about the time his father was quitting the ring.'

Anthony Martin Sinatra, Frank's father, had been a bantamweight who never made it beyond local semi-finals; he boxed under the name Marty O'Brien because in those days an Irish name was absolutely necessary for prize fighters if they wanted to draw the fans. Relatives and neighbours remembered him as a quiet man. 'Dolly was always the go-getter', a brother-in-law said. 'She was the brains of the family. But there was never any conflict. Marty agreed with Dolly and he was happy to take a back seat to her.'

After leaving the ring, Marty Sinatra worked for a time as a boilermaker. When he lost that job, Dolly raised the money (a loan from her mother) that enabled him to open his tavern. When she had attained a degree of local political power, as a committeewoman, she got her husband an appointment as captain in the local fire department. Until his death in 1968, Marty Sinatra was always called 'Captain'.

But Dolly Sinatra actually ruled her family; her rank was always well above that of the Captain. Marty, say friends who knew the Sinatras, was relatively weak and unambitious;

he bowed to his wife's wishes and he owed both his tavern business and his fire department rank to his wife's driving spirit. What effect this role reversal may have had on Sinatra will probably never be known. But the tradition of a domineering father and a mother who never leaves kitchen and children is stronger among Sicilians than even mainland Italians and other Mediterranean ethnic groups. Friends claim to see some of that effect on the adult Sinatra. One actress who dated Frank a number of times in the late Fifties told me, 'Frank was charming, and all the scandal magazine stuff about his being a fabulous lover was absolute truth. Not only physically, but psychically. He knew how to make a woman feel like a woman. But after a while he would seem to demand that you be the good Italian housewife and hang around to take care of his needs while he was off with his friends, that you be home at the phone until he was ready for you again. You know he discouraged his first wife, Nancy, from remarrying? Well, after getting to know Frank I came to believe that Nancy was almost a mother figure to him, the woman who would be at home to take care of his kids and to cook his dinner a couple of times a week – which I hear she still does – and to provide the solid roots, the family base, that he may have missed as a kid. You know Dolly wasn't around that much when he was a child? She was working or politicking when Frank was growing up. I've often wondered what effect that had on a kid with such a strong Italian heritage.'

When Dolly was first getting into politics, Frank spent week-ends with his baby sitter, Mrs Carrier, and the rest of his time in the care of his maternal grandmother, Mrs Rosa Garaventi, in her grocery store. Later, after the grandmother died, Frank found a part-time substitute mother in an elderly Jewish woman who is remembered by neighbours only as Mrs Golden. (In later years, Sinatra has sometimes worn the Jewish religious symbol, a mezzuzah, around his neck, given to him by Mrs Golden according to friends. He's also given friends medallions with a St Christopher on one side and a Star of David on the other.)

Dolly gave Frank a great deal of love during the time she

did spend with him – he was her only child and was 'spoiled' say the children he grew up with – and she implanted in him a fighting spirit.

'I don't know where the stories about Frank being tough and always fighting with kids might come from', his former babysitter said. 'If he did fight – and I never saw it – it was because he was pretty skinny and some of the kids used to pick on him. I remember once when he was about 7 or 8, he came up crying after somebody on the street had hit him. His mother spanked him a little, then chased him back into the street. "Go fight your own battles, Frank", she said. She took care of him a lot, but she always taught him independence. She never went out to fight his battles for him; she made him fight back.'

Probably in imitation of his mother, Sinatra quite early developed his lifelong habit of buying gifts for his friends. His family, while not wealthy, prospered because of Dolly's political connections and political largesse, and as an only child, Frank got everything he demanded from his mother, while his friends had few possessions because they all had between six and a dozen or so siblings.

'Frank always had whatever he needed', Mrs Carrier recalls. 'He was the best dressed kid on the block and he always had the newest gadgets and toys. Later on, in his teens, his mother always used to take him to the Catskills, or maybe to Long Branch on the Jersey shore, for two or three weeks every summer. He was the only kid on the block ever to get away for a vacation. And he always had a lot of clothes – no one else around here owned clothes like his.'

Other old friends say Frank had a wardrobe of suits, trousers, and sports coats that seemed as complete as a man's furnishings store compared to what the other kids owned. 'He had so many pairs of pants that they called him "Slacksy" ', a childhood friend said. And he constantly gave his clothing away to anyone who seemed to envy or praise a particular item. He had a charge account at the only department store in town and he occasionally bought clothing for his friends. Once, when he was 16 and dating the sister of one of his friends, they all planned a sweet sixteen party for Frank's girl. But one of the boys in the crowd didn't have any clothes for the party, so Frank bought him a complete outfit.

'Somebody once said that Frank considers himself *Il Padrone*', another childhood friend said years later. 'Well, I can believe that from all I've heard. And I think it started because his mother was the politician giving out presents and his father was a nobody who didn't care that he was a nobody. I think that's where it all started. Frank had to show that one of the Sinatra men was going to command a lot of respect from everybody in the world. Not that his father wasn't respected. He was. He ran the tavern and he was on the fire department. But he was just a quiet guy compared to Frank's mother, and some people used to say that Dolly pushed him around. That's one of the things that makes Sinatra tick, in my opinion, that he was going to get a lot more respect than his father did.'

It has often been said that Sinatra always felt like an underdog – Frank has said it himself – a member of a repressed minority group. That feeling, which has led to so many violent physical assaults on people who have crossed him, was no doubt nurtured in the Sicilian-Italian ghetto in which he was raised.

It must be remembered that when Sinatra was a child most immigrants, and especially Italians, felt they were mistreated by those who held power in their adopted land. In the early Twenties, a national insanity called the Red Scare swept the nation. Radicals, many of them Italian, were arrested, beaten, and deported by a Federal government that was ostensibly attempting to cleanse American society of Communists and other flag-burners, but that was actually trying to break up the union movement. At least one Italian radical, undergoing 'questioning' by Federal police in a New York City building, was thrown from a window and killed, murdered by agents who claimed most naturally that the man died while 'attempting to escape'. And a few years later, Sacco and Vanzetti were convicted on manufactured evidence and executed for a murder they probably never committed.

The feeling in the Italian ghettoes was quite strong: American society was intent on destroying every immigrant, but especially an Italian, who attempted to protest against the suppression of workers' legitimate demands and who tried to climb from the ghetto. Years after the Red Scare, when Fiorello La Guardia was mayor of New York City and Italians were beginning to feel they were finding a place in a once-hostile society, I remember several elderly Italian neighbours commenting on Sinatra's phenomenal fame: '*They* finally allowed an Italian to get big and famous. *They* murdered Valentino and Columbo. . . .' It didn't matter to them that, officially, Rudolph Valentino had died of a ruptured appendix and popular singer Russ Columbo was killed in an accidental shooting. The immigrants knew that *They* had murdered these Italians just as *They* had killed so many others who had refused to be docile and stay in their place. That attitude, so prevalent between the two world wars, definitely had some basis in fact. The American experience has always been that the latest immigrant group has been abused and exploited until it becomes assimilated in the second and third generation. And the common experience of exploitation led immigrants of all nationalities to band together in self-protection against an American society they could not understand. Sinatra's parents were members of the Sicilian Cultural League even though both had been totally Americanized and had made a place for themselves in the local political structure.

Other immigrants banded together in the Mafia. During the Prohibition years the men of the Mafia were, on the whole, applauded by immigrants who would have wept and lit candles to the Virgin Mary had their son become *mafiosi*; though the Italian and Sicilian immigrants feared those gangsters, there arose, even in the honest and hardworking members of the ghetto, a sense of pride that some of their number, even though criminal, were learning to bend the system to their will. For many, especially young men like Frank, the *uomini respettati* of the Mafia were romantic figures, Robin Hoods of America. Sinatra wanted to be known as a tough street fighter. 'Frank was a tough kid, because he never was afraid', his Uncle Dom Garaventi told me years ago. 'I remember when he was about twelve, I was standing on the corner of Fifth and Grand talking to a couple of friends and Frank came riding by on his bike. He accidentally ran into a kid who crossed in front of him. Pretty soon four or five kids were whacking the tar out of him. But he wasn't afraid. He just stood up to them and traded punches and never backed down until they all got tired and the fighting just stopped. He had lots of fights as a kid, because he had a temper. But he was never a bully. He just wasn't going to let anybody push him around.' The tough street fighters of Frank's ethnic background – Al Capone, Lucky Luciano, and especially Willie Moretti, the local Mafia boss who was a major influence in New Jersey politics – had been made famous and wealthy by Prohibition and were men of respect. Sinatra, in a way, both respected and emulated them. He would be respected by his own peer group through his generosity, or with his fists.

'All the talent Frank got, he got from my father', said Uncle Dom Garaventi. 'Pop had a tremendous voice, he was a great singer. I remember when Frank was just a kid, all the relatives used to come out from Brooklyn and New York on a Sunday. There'd be lots of food and wine, and Pop would sing. Dolly, too, used to sing at weddings and other family affairs. Like in most Italian families in those days, Frank just grew up with a lot of music around him, good music, real music.'

With remarkable foresight, Garaventi bought young Frank a ukelele when he was about fifteen – 'the year he met Nancy Barbato, the first girl he ever took an interest in and the first girl who ever took an interest in him' – and he learned to play it mostly to serenade Nancy. He was the only kid in the neighbourhood with a musical instrument, and that summer he sat under the lamp post in front of his house, strumming it constantly and singing Crosby and Columbo songs. Nancy and all the others around would sit with him, fascinated that he was learning to play it.

Frank soon became involved with a teenage band and

they'd get week-end jobs, weddings, and anniversary celebrations. Most of their time was spent practising in the club rooms of the Georgie Harper Association, a political club housed in a building owned by one of Frank's uncles. There was a stage and a drum and piano in the club, and Frank and his boys would practise every afternoon, Frank strumming his uke and singing; the instrument was, at that time, more important than the singing. But as Frank's aunt, Josephine Monaco, later recalled, 'A short time after Frank started going out steady with Nancy, he took her into New York to the Paramount to see Bing Crosby. I think it was the summer he was seventeen. And after Crosby went off the stage Frank turned to Nancy and said, "I'm going to be a singer." When they got home that night he announced it, very seriously, "I'm going to be a singer." We asked what he meant and he said, "I saw Bing Crosby tonight and I've got to be a singer." I remember it like it was yesterday.' And Garaventi remembered, 'Then he started singing with the combo and before you knew it he didn't want to be a musician anymore, but a singer.'

Despite his official biographies, which later said his parents were aghast at the idea, there was no real opposition. Frank had already quit high school after forty-seven days attendance and got a job loading newspapers on trucks at the old *Jersey Observer*. But it was decided that he was too frail for such strenuous work so he was made a copyboy. For a time, until he saw Bing perform, he had dreamed of being a sportswriter. But now he took to walking through the streets of Hoboken, wearing a plaid sports jacket and singing into the unlit pipe in his mouth, as Crosby did.

The band broke up after a while, but Sinatra continued to sing every chance he got, including a six-month unpaid stint at a local radio station, a job Uncle Garaventi got for him through political contacts after Frank said some radio experience would help him become more professional. In 1934, when he was nineteen, Sinatra began ingratiating himself with a group called the Three Flashes – local lorry drivers, all a few years older than Frank, who were then singing at week-ends at the Rustic Cabin.

'Frank hung around us like we were gods or something', remembers Fred Tamburro, a member of the group. 'We took him along for one simple reason: Frankie-boy had a car. He used to chauffeur us around.' One night a promoter approached them at the Rustic Cabin and said he wanted the Three Flashes to make some movie shorts as an audition for Major Bowes, who had grown wealthy and famous with his radio and road-show programme, the Amateur Hour. When Frank heard about it, he pestered and begged them to take him into the group and turn it into a quarter. Fred and the other two Flashes, James Petrozelli (called Sky by Sinatra) and Patty Principi, turned Frank down. Dolly Sinatra asked them to at least audition her son. They did.

'We took him on because he improved us', Sky said years later. 'There was no pressure from his mother or anything like that. We just sounded better as four.' Other residents of Hoboken who were around in those days later recalled that Dolly Sinatra indeed put the pressure on the Three Flashes, that she used all her charm to get Frank accepted in the group; Tamburro admitted they took Frank on because Dolly was so influential.

In any case, the new Hoboken Four, as they called themselves, made a couple of shorts for the Major Bowes organization and were selected as contestants on the Amateur Hour. Their debut was broadcast from the stage of New York's Capitol Theatre on 8th September 1935, with Frank as lead singer. A gadget to measure applause from the audience and phone call votes from at-home listeners gave the Hoboken Four the first prize. They were then made part of a Major Bowes travelling unit, at fifty dollars a week plus meals. Even back then Frank was singled out as something special. During a tour stopover in Oakland, California, the band leader at a posh nightclub asked Frank to get up and sing. He did, without any kind of rehearsal with the band, and the audience wouldn't let him leave the stage. 'What the hell are you doing in a quartet?' the band leader asked.

By that time Frank was wondering the same thing, but not necessarily for professional reasons. Recalls one member of Major Bowes Touring Unit No. One, 'Almost from the beginning Frank stood out as the best in the group. He did a lot of solos and he got a lot of attention from Bowes and the other executives running the thing. A couple of members of the Hoboken Four resented it and began to push Frank around, because he had become the star of the entire unit.

'After the show, people would flock backstage and just about mob Frank. The others would be asked to sign an autograph or two, but Frank was practically torn apart. He'd have to fight off the nicest women you've ever seen. All the women ever wanted was to climb into bed with Frank Sinatra, even though he was just a kid. It used to gripe at two members of his group especially; they had to work to get their women, but Frank just had to open his mouth, croon a little song, and have more women than he could handle in a month.

'Two of the members of his quartet started getting in the habit of beating Frank every once in a while, whenever they got mad at something and had to take it out on someone. It happened often enough so that you could call it abuse. They abused Frank, and it happened most often when Frank went off with some woman after the show and these two no-talents had to go to their rooms alone to whack off.

'I remember one real bad night, just a short time before Frank left us. They were singing on stage and one guy in the group – the one who didn't pick on Frank – started to giggle. He caught himself after a while and got back into the harmony but then Frank started it. Pretty soon they were all giggling and the curtain had to be run down.

'They went back to their dressing room and waited for Major Bowes to come and bawl them out. One of the group began yelling at Frank: "What are you, crazy?" Frank was still smiling about it all and he said, "I can't help it, that's my sense of humour." I'll never forget it. Frank was sitting on an old wardrobe trunk, one leg crossed over the other. One of the guys who always beat him up rushed over, screaming, "Well, here's my sense of humour", and he let Frank have a solid right that sent him flying off his trunk and onto the floor in a heap. Frank picked himself up, looked at the guy, then just turned and walked out. He went back to Hoboken a few days later.'

A member of the Hoboken Four, who would not permit his name to be used, confirmed the abuse. 'Sometimes it got pretty bad for Frank', he said. 'After all, he was a skinny little guy and the two picking on him were older and bigger, truck drivers back home, and Frank couldn't fight back. Once we were sitting in a diner, stretched in a line along the counter. Frank leaned over and whispered to me, "Why don't you beat me too and make it unanimous?" I shrugged him off. I felt real bad about it and I still do, but what could I have done back then?'

Even then, an amateur in name only because Major Bowes ran a totally professional production, Sinatra seemed absolutely dedicated to his future career. Recalls the member of the group Frank nicknamed Sky, 'It wasn't that his voice was so great, at the beginning. Mostly it was that he had his heart and soul in it. He wouldn't stop; he always wanted to practice, always wanted to rehearse. That's one of the reasons he got so good after just a couple of months on tour. It was eerie sometimes. I remember we used to travel by bus from city to city, one-night stands. The bus would be packed, people talking, people necking, people reading — everything people do on a bus. Then Frank would start to sing from somewhere down back and everything stopped. Things got so quiet in that damned bus that a pin sounded like a bomb. That kid really had it.'

The member of the old Hoboken Four who did *not* beat Frank during the tour days says of the two who did, 'They continued being lousy to Frank even after he started making it with Tommy Dorsey. One of the reasons Frank really hates Hoboken and got his parents out of there as soon as he could afford to buy them a house is that a lot of jealous people in Hoboken really mistreated him. One day when he was at the Paramount with Dorsey, the guys who used to beat him went up and tried to borrow money from him. Frank wasn't making that much, he was still struggling, and he turned them down — especially since they used to treat him so bad.

'After that they went around spreading stories about Frank. They started the rumour that he was a draft dodger during the war, that he didn't have anything wrong with his ears like the Army said but bought his way out. They said he had bastard kids all over the country. They even said he had TB. One of them used that line when he used to emcee in a little club. If the audience didn't cheer when he came on stage he would say, "What did you expect? Frank Sinatra? Well, Sinatra's TB finally caught up with him so he won't be here tonight. You got me instead." And then the guy used to tell people that it was the truth, Frank was sick from TB.'

As Frank Sinatra was slowly developing into the enormous sensation that he would become, he seemed also to develop a large amount of self-confidence that appeared to some to be conceit, to others to be mere youthful cockiness, and to still others to be arrogance.

The self-confidence was evident as early as his first weeks with Harry James. A *Down Beat* reporter interviewing James after a show asked the band leader, 'Who's that skinny little singer? He sings a great song.' James shot back, 'Not so loud. The kid's name is Sinatra. He considers himself the greatest vocalist in the business. Get that! No one has ever heard of him. He's never had a hit record. He looks like a wet rag. But he says he's the greatest. If he hears you compliment him he'll demand a raise tonight.'

But one member of the James band may have put his finger on the truth behind Sinatra's cockiness when he said years later, 'The kid knew he was good, no doubt about it. But the cockiness was really just a front. I remember a number of times Frank was so depressed that the band wasn't shooting into the sky, that he wasn't becoming a big star, he actually talked about quitting. The guy who talked him out of it all the time was Hank Sanicola. He used to be a fighter, then became a song-plugger, and after Frank became the biggest thing in music, he made Sanicola practically his partner. Hank persuaded Frank to keep going.

'What it really came down to, I'm pretty sure, is that Frank used the cockiness and the arrogance to hide his fear of failing, used it as a mask because he wasn't really convinced he was as good as everybody said he was. He had as much fear of failing as any guy in show business ever had, but he just wasn't going to let anybody see it because he was too proud.'

Perhaps Sinatra's insecurities in the face of the most incredible public adulation ever given any performer may be at least a partial explanation for his constant, although unspoken, demand for respect. It's a guess, pure speculation, but after months of researching this man, I am left with the very strong feeling that his *Il Padrone* attitude, his public brawls, and private vendettas, his close association with real-life mafia godfathers, his lack of compulsion that Nancy cited – all the conflicting, 'schizophrenic' (to use Cheshire's rather careless word) behaviour by Frank Sinatra is a form of defence enabling him to avoid facing himself.

On a few rare occasions, Frank has come close to admitting that his fears and insecurities may be the unconscious motivation behind his erratic behaviour, but then he's backed away from such potentially dangerous self-analysis.

'Like a fighter, I've got all the help I need before the bout', Frank said a number of years ago. 'But when the bell rings, I go it alone. There's no one I can turn to except myself. Take a fellow who works in business, makes a product. *I'm* my product. Every time I go on a sound stage or into a recording session I've got nothing working for me except myself. I get sick, I'm out of business. I cut a few bad records, I'm out of business. I do a bad job on a couple of films, I'm out of business.

'I'm not copping a plea for sympathy. I've got a lot going for me, but I'm human, too. I'm afraid sometimes of the unknown, of the thing I may not be prepared for. And after going it alone all day, I have to go it alone afterwards. Loneliness is pretty much forced on an entertainer. . . .'

The pain that Sinatra was showing in that remark, and the fact that he quickly changed the subject before the interviewer could probe more deeply, is rather significant. Outwardly self-assured and occasionally filled with brash arrogance, seemingly in charge of his friends and his fans, inwardly Sinatra appears to be filled with fears that he seldom admits to.

He doesn't have the time. He doesn't want to make the time. For, as so many of his friends have pointed out over the years, Sinatra will work from late morning until late at night, play and play very hard until all the joints have shut down and all his friends have collapsed from weariness, then read until dawn – 'Because he hates to be with himself', as one friend has put it.

Frank has admittedly built a defence around his psyche to keep out intrusions that could hurt, a defence that at the same time enables him to lock *in* the insecurities he doesn't want to face. As his daughter, Nancy, once said, 'Daddy says that when you get to be his age, you've built a wall of asbestos around you so that things don't flake you out like they once did.'

CHAPTER 3

'I've often had the strong feeling that Frank Sinatra, Hollywood's great lover, doesn't really like women very much', says an actress who once dated Sinatra regularly.

A number of women, and men, who know Sinatra have come to the same conclusion. They'll tell you that the most obvious evidence of what Frank really thinks of women is the extensive vocabulary of unflattering words he uses to describe them, such as 'broad', which has always been his favourite. He doesn't seem to understand that the word offends many women, that a young woman like Mia Farrow, his wife of four weeks, might cry because he called her a 'broad' in front of a large nightclub crowd.

An actress who had once been a column item because of her romance with Sinatra told me, 'That word isn't just something he uses as a gag or out of habit from his Hoboken days. It really seems to sum up his entire attitude toward women. The men around him are the guys, his boys. The women aren't even people. They're all broads.

'Don't get me wrong. He's very charming. When you're alone with him, Frank makes you feel as if you're the only woman in the world. He's the perfect lover that way, turning his full attention and charm on you.

'But when he's in front of his jock friends he behaves differently. He'll do something like turn to one of his *paisans* and say, "See if the broad wants some sauce...."'

Another woman had a brief encounter with Sinatra that she'll remember the rest of her life, although Sinatra probably forgot it the moment it ended. The woman is a young executive in a branch of the entertainment industry in New

York. One night a couple of years ago a friend from Hollywood came to town and took her to dinner. Later, he asked her to accompany him to the East Side apartment that his brother, a film executive, maintained for business.

'He had to pick up some papers and things for his brother', the woman recalls. 'So we went up there and let ourselves in with his set of keys. There were four or five people in the apartment and I didn't know what was going on. But my date recognized the men, and he simply explained to a man who was lying on the couch, surrounded by tough-looking men, that he was on an errand for his brother. And he went off to his brother's study.

'I didn't recognize the man on the couch at first, but the minute he spoke I knew it was Sinatra. He said to one of his protectors, "See if the broad wants some sauce." I didn't know what kind of sauce he was talking about until his friend asked me if I wanted a drink. I said no thank you. Sinatra said, "See if the broad wants a bite to eat." His friend passed the question to me and I said no. Sinatra kept on with it, but he never spoke directly to me. Always, "See if the broad wants. . . ." Finally he said, "I guess the broad doesn't want a damn thing", and he turned around on the couch as if he'd been insulted.

'When we finally left I kept thinking, "I don't know whether I'm more upset that he called me a broad, or never spoke to me directly, or that I didn't know sauce meant liquor." '

Those of his older friends who would talk about Sinatra agree that he has always had a somewhat coarse attitude toward women. But, they report, it grew coarser after his marriage to Ava Gardner broke up.

'Frank was badly hurt by Ava', says one Hollywood director who has drifted in and out of Sinatra's circle over the years and who, like so many, would talk only if his name were not used because he'd like to drift in again some day. 'He felt that she raked him over publicly. She kept chasing around with Dominguin and other bullfighters, with Italian actors, with a few Englishmen, and a lot of her affairs made headlines.

'That hurt a man of his ego, a man who still possesses that old-fashioned Sicilian attitude about a woman staying at home and keeping her place. I don't think Frank was as upset about her running around as he was about the headlines and some of her nasty cracks about him, because she made him look like a cuckold. But even more important than that, after Frank publicly broke up his own marriage and acted like a schoolboy over Ava – the Don Juan of our age freaking out over a broad like any teenager would – the marriage went bad and she dumped him. That hurt. Mostly because, I believe, Frank felt he was a failure in the one thing in his life that really mattered at the time, Ava Gardner. For a man of his fragile sensibility, that was as tough as the empty seats in the theatres and nightclubs. Ava was a personal failure, which inside is even worse than a professional one.

'After Ava I don't think he ever trusted or respected a woman again. Except for his first wife, Nancy, who's been more like a mother than a former wife. And maybe Barbara Marx, in the beginning.'

'When Frank first started out he wore his heart on his sleeve', one of the people who knew him best in the early Hollywood days told a writer some years back. 'Even today (in 1960), as cold and calculating and hard as he can be, he still wears his heart on his sleeve. For this reason, he gets hurt very easily.'

When I contacted that man fifteen years later and asked whether he felt the same way, he laughed. 'Not only doesn't Frank show the heart any more, he doesn't even let you see the sleeve. He's grown a lot more insulated and a lot more reclusive, and even the people closest to him never know what he's *really* feeling, inside. Sure, they'll see him be angry and lash out, or feel sorry for someone in trouble and start writing cheques to help, but what's in his heart is known only to Sinatra. I think Sinatra knows it, I hope he does, but sometimes you get the feeling he's blocked it all so that nobody can see it, so that only *he* can see it in those wee small hours when he's finally alone and forced to face it.'

Another old Sinatra friend, an actress speaking, like so

many, only after the promise to anonymity, told me, 'When you start writing about Frank and his women, there's something very important to keep in mind. Put aside for a minute all the stories about how well-hung he is, how great a lover he is, how he romances a woman with such intensity that she can easily believe she's the only woman in the world. All that's true. But there's something more vital to the man that so many people have overlooked.

'Sinatra is an artist. I mean that sincerely. Sure, he says he's just a saloon singer. But he is as much an artist as Caruso was, as Picasso, as Blake. Sinatra *feels*, Sinatra absorbs and then synthesizes what he's absorbed through the filters of his crazy brain until it comes out something special. That's what made him a great singer and great performer, as superb in his field as any other artist working in any medium. Frank feels pain, he *feels* everything, and it almost drives him *crazy* because most of us don't feel what he feels. He's an outsider.'

'Colin Wilson's *Outsider*?' I asked.

'You know the book? Then you know what I'm talking about. The outsider is an abnormal person in our society. When he's the average kind of man, perhaps working in a shop, with no channel into any of the arts, then he's simply considered a nut and either kept in line by his relatives or his psychiatrist or, in some cases, he's committed. But when he writes poetry, paints, is a novelist or a sculptor – or a singer like Sinatra – then his madness goes into his art, it's synthesized in his brain and comes out something special and. . . .'

'We were discussing Sinatra and his women', I reminded her.

'That's the point I'm leading up to. Sinatra's women have never been the most important thing in his life. The most important thing, above anything else, has been his art. Those who don't understand Sinatra will say it's his *career* that's most important, as if it were an ego thing. "Sinatra has to be the best and the greatest", I heard somebody say at one of those awful Hollywood parties. And everybody nodded, right, ego, a need for fame, and all that nonsense. It isn't that. It's a need for self-expression, the artist's need to put into his art everything he feels so deeply and would go insane with it bottled inside him. He is completely wrapped up in his art. And the women have always had to take a second place to the art. The one time that wasn't true was when he started chasing Ava. He pushed his art aside for a woman and he suffered for it, as an artist. That won't ever again happen to Sinatra.'

In a conversation later reported by a *Look* magazine writer, young Frank Sinatra, singing at the Rustic Cabin and going steady for the previous three years with Nancy Barbato, is supposed to have said to her, 'I'm going to the top and I don't want anyone dragging on my neck.'

To which Nancy is said to have replied, 'I won't get in your way, Frank.'

Whether or not the story is true – and it has been repeated often enough so that it now assumes the forces of Holy Writ in all stories about Sinatra – they were married on 4th February 1939. Almost immediately, Harry James hired him and Sinatra, true to his word, started going to the top.

Years later, Sinatra said his marriage began to fall apart after its first year, despite the birth of their first child, Nancy Sandra. There were several forces creating friction in the marriage. Nancy argued constantly with Sinatra's mother, Dolly, who apparently tried to run her son's household the way she ran her own, with intense domination. Then, too, Frank was constantly annoyed about all the other Barbatos who seemed to infiltrate his household, and he occasionally complained that his wife's relatives were leeches.

But most of all, Sinatra appeared to have second thoughts about having married a childhood sweetheart who didn't seem to fit into the world of glamour, and glamorous women, in which he found himself. Touring with the James band, Frank once more had his pick of the women in every city in which they played.

'He seemed to have an unsatisfiable appetite for women', a member of the Harry James band said later.

And then he went to Hollywood, leaving his wife behind in their new home in Hasbrouck Heights, New Jersey, expect-

Frank and
Nancy Sinatra at
a film premier
in 1946

Below:
Frank greets
Dolly Sinatra,
his mother

Sinatra announces his plans
to marry Ava Gardner;
this, and the happy photograph, right, of the couple,
married in 1951, give little
indication of the stormy
relationship that was to
follow

At a Royal Film Premier in London in October
1958, Sinatra is presented to the Queen. Below, a
less formal London get-together at Shepperton
Studios in August 1961: from left to right, Bing
Crosby, Sinatra, Dean Martin and Bob Hope

In a jovial mood at
a recording session,
June 1962

Frank's parents on
their fiftieth
wedding anni-
versary, New
Jersey 1963

By the mid 1950s, Sinatra
was the most adored
singing idol in the world.
His children were not slow
to follow in his footsteps:
below left, Sinatra's
singing daughter Nancy
with her mother, Frank's
first wife; below right,
Frank Sinatra Jr,
rehearsing a show in
London 1964

In 1954, still early days in his film career, Sinatra won a coveted Oscar for his part as Maggio, the ill-fated GI in 'From Here To Eternity' (above)

Sinatra in a scene from 'Von Ryan's Express', 1964

Sinatra dated a host of
good-looking women,
between, and some-
times during his
marriages, and they
have been a source of
constant speculation.
Above, Sinatra and
Natalie Wood at the
Hollywood premier of
'My Fair Lady', 1964;
below, Las Vegas, 1966,
the fifty-year-old singer
married twenty-one-
year-old Mia Farrow,
star of 'Peyton Place'

Frank out on the town
with Jacqueline Onassis,
September 1975

Right:Frank with Barbara
Marx in May 1976;
they were married in July

ing their second child (who would be named Franklin in honour of the President). The story goes that the first thing Frank did when he got settled into his dressing room at the RKO studios was to tack on the wall a list of at least two dozen of the most beauteous Hollywood stars; by the time the film, *Higher and Higher*, was completed, a check mark of conquest was beside almost every name.

True or not, Sinatra was involved with, or reported to be involved with, more women than even the Aga Khan, acknowledged by most gossips to have been the international sexual champion. Among Frank's conquests, real or simply gossip, have been Lana Turner, Marilyn Maxwell, Marilyn Monroe, Marlene Dietrich, Gloria Vanderbilt, Kim Novak, Lauren Bacall, Anita Ekberg, Judy Garland, Nan Whitney, Natalie Wood, Jill St John, Debbie Reynolds, Sophia Loren, Gina Lollobrigida, Shirley MacLaine . . . the list would go on and on.

Humphrey Bogart, one of Frank's great friends in Hollywood, once said of him, 'I don't think Frank's an adult emotionally. He can't settle down.' Another time Bogart remarked, 'Frank's idea of paradise is a place where there are plenty of women and no newspapermen. He doesn't realize it, but he'd be bettter off if it were the other way around.'

But the women who were drawn to Sinatra back then had a different view of the man. Deborah Kerr once told a writer, 'There's a curiously tender and vulnerable quality about Frank. That is what touches his audience – and it wants to touch back.' Judy Garland, saying almost the same thing, didn't think it necessary to move away from Frank and into the audience when she told a writer, 'You want to take care of him. I regard Frank as my extra child.'

Writer Richard Gehman reports that a friend of Sinatra at that time told him, 'Frank was in Hollywood, Nancy was in New Jersey. Nearly every day Frank was reported in the columns as being out with some actress. Nancy would call George Evans, his press agent and closest friend. George would try to explain that the reports didn't mean anything, that press agents tried to get space for their female clients by handing out false reports, by saying that they were seen with Sinatra. There would be more column items. Nancy would call George again. George would call Frank. Frank would say, "Go out and buy her a present or something, for God's sake", and George would then have to take Nancy shopping.'

Soon after Frank moved to the West Coast he began seeing much of Lana Turner, who was working on the same studio lot. George Evans tried to caution Frank that his fans would be furious, but he wouldn't listen; he didn't seem to understand that his open flouting of convention, even in Hollywood, was shocking people and could turn his fans against him should the press begin to inquire a little more deeply. The nearest Frank came to trying to maintain a facade was on the numerous occasions he and Lana would appear in public with Evans, who pretended she was his date.

The romance with Lana soon broke up – some say because she was more interested in Howard Hughes – and he began to concentrate on Marilyn Maxwell. 'Frank was ready to leave Nancy for Marilyn', a friend says. Although he didn't leave his wife, Sinatra appeared to be doing everything possible to force her to leave him. He took Marilyn to New York with him in 1946 to see the Joe Louis-Billy Conn heavyweight championship in a stadium where 20,000 fans including hundreds of newspapermen, would see him and the sexy blond. Toots Shor talked him out of that one – and Marlene Dietrich turned up at Frank's side at the fight.

Nancy, by now living in the Beverly Hills house that Frank had brought (she still lives in it today), somehow put up with the humiliation of reading about her husband's exploits and hearing about them from the bitchy gossips of Hollywood. After all, Frank did come home to her and their children. He did need her and she loved him. However, the humiliation sometimes struck deep. Once, according to a former Sinatra associate, Nancy had given him one of her rings to drop off at the jeweller's to be cleaned and repaired, a ring that had been a present from Frank. He put it into his pocket and the next time Nancy saw it was during a party at the Sinatra home. It was on the finger of a lovely blonde showgirl invited to the party by Frank. Nancy later told a friend, 'I felt so humiliated, I thought I would kill myself.'

It was Sinatra's publicity, and his publicity man, who kept him from leaving Nancy for another woman on several occasions. Evans, it is said, broke up his relationship with Marilyn Maxwell. Evans, according to Hollywood insiders, helped convinced Sinatra that Lana Turner was simply using him to make Howard Hughes jealous. Whenever Frank seemed to get really serious over a Hollywood showgirl – a distinction often made to separate those few serious romances from the much more numerous affairs that were simply sexual – George Evans found some way to bring Frank back to reality.

But then Frank met Ava, and he fell in love, to use his own inadequate words for the reaction that flashed between them. And once he met Ava, none of his friends or advisers could talk any sense into him.

Frank and Ava had met years earlier and Frank had come on to her, but Ava refused to become simply another conquest of this skinny kid from Hoboken with the conquest list on his dressing room door. She had more self-esteem than most Hollywood women who've come through the film studio levelling and couch-casting process of star-building.

'Ava disliked Frank intensely', Ruth Rosenthal, one of her friends at the time, later told writer Charles Higham. 'She kept saying that she found him conceited, arrogant, and overpowering. They had an instant hostility.'

When they did come together finally, after bumping into one another at the opening of the Broadway musical, *Gentlemen Prefer Blondes*, in December, 1949, something flashed between them and they went off together for the night. And for the next several days. When they did emerge from wherever they spent their very private moments together, it was to make the scene at several night spots. Their romance became the talk of the town, the New York gossip columnists filling the newspapers and the airwaves with questions, because they had no answers.

Frank didn't see Ava again until a couple of weeks later

at a party in Palm Springs. They left together, early. Driving her home, Frank stopped on the way and sang to her under a palm tree, and both laughed wildly at the charming, absurdly romantic gesture. The next day they rode through nearby towns, Frank firing a pistol out the window of his car at the joy of their having discovered one another.

'Frank wasn't just in love with her', a friend said later. 'He was simply *obsessed* by her.'

As Ava's biographer, Charles Higham, has written: 'They were drawn to each other not only because of sexual attraction but because they were so much alike. Both were night people, barely capable of sleeping at all, liking to sit up into the small hours. Both loved Italian food, hard liquor, boxing matches; both were generous, warm, fiercely honest, violent-tempered, afraid of being used, deeply insecure and sceptical of their own talents, neurotic, tension-ridden. Their energies fused, and their relationship was from the outset passionate and yet deeply frustrating, tormenting because, similar as they were, they had a terrifying ability to seek out each other's weaknesses.' Like Frank, Ava was the kind of person who always had to be on the move because she was afraid to sit still and think, and perhaps begin to face up to herself.

By now Sinatra's popularity had begun to dip, ever so slightly, as a younger crop of singer-belters began to stir the newest group of bobby-soxers, as they were still called. There was talk in the trade papers about Frank 'slipping', and criticism of some of his recordings. But his acting in *On The Town* (which had its premiere in New York the night after he and Ava came together) received almost universal acclaim, and the film brought in a bigger box-office gross in its first weeks than any other in Radio City Music Hall's history.

Still, his recordings in this period were beginning to sound dull, listless, and forced; Sinatra sounded as if he were tired of it all after seven years as an international sensation. Most important of all, Frank seemed to be losing his grip on himself, seemed to be more openly frightened about his professional future, appearing almost 'desperate' to some friends because 'he thought his old magic was deserting him'.

Back in Beverly Hills for the Christmas holidays with his wife and children – his third, Tina, had been born the year before – Frank signed a contract to appear for two weeks at the Shamrock Hotel in Houston, beginning 28th January 1950. Just a few days before the opening, the one man who seemed able to curb Frank's apparent need to publicly proclaim his bachelorhood despite wife and three children, George Evans, dropped dead of a heart attack shortly after defending Frank in a violent argument with a newspaper writer. Frank postponed his Shamrock opening to fly to the funeral in New York. 'For Frank', said songwriter Jimmy Van Heusen, 'the sudden death of George Evans was an emotional shock that defies words.' It was much more than that : It removed probably the most important moderating influence on Frank's behaviour.

Without Evans to guide him, as he had so skillfully done during periods of conflict with the press and numerous romances, Frank invited Ava to fly with him to Houston. 'A major mistake', he later admitted. 'But I was so in love I didn't care how it looked, having her there while I was still married.'

The gossip items ballooned into headlines the first night of Frank's engagement at the Shamrock. He and Ava dined at a small Italian restaurant after the show, the guests of Houston's mayor, who called the press. When a photographer asked whether he could take a picture, Frank refused. Either the photographer politely walked away (Frank's version) or Sinatra threatened to punch him in the nose and had him ejected from the restaurant (the newspaper's version). The latter account is what was published across the country.

A couple of weeks later Hollywood columnist Hedda Hopper reported that Sinatra had moved out of his Beverly Hills home and that Nancy had confirmed the separation – their third in three years – but said there were no plans for divorce. Immediately, the Sinatra-Ava affair became an illicit romance in the press, and Frank was so mindlessly in love that he gave reporters more copy than even they could have hoped for.

In March, Frank arrived in New York City to play his

first date at the Copacabana in years. He checked into the Hampshire House, overlooking Central Park. Hours later, Ava Gardner checked into an equally luxurious suite on another floor. Hours after that, the newspapers announced in wartime headlines. FRANK & AVA AT SAME HOTEL. Central Park South became a camping ground for reporters and photographers. Frank made matters worse when, a week before his Copa opening, he got into an argument with Faye Emerson, who was to play Queen to his King at a benefit ball for the Red Cross. Frank arrived very late at a publicity photo session for the ball, and Miss Emerson, made late for a TV rehearsal, snapped, 'Big Shot! I'll be damned if I'm going to pose with you.' Sinatra shouted back, using much stronger words than damn, according to the newspapers which were too genteel to publish the expletives. But not so genteel that they could resist implying Frank was late because he was shacked up with Hurricane Ava, as they began calling her. The night of the ball, Sinatra failed to appear; the papers reported he went out nightclubbing with Ava.

And a torrent of vile and abusive letters began pouring into the Hampshire House, most of them addressed to Ava and most of them calling her an assortment of variations on the term *whore*. She told Frank that she was going to fly to London to escape the pressures. He begged her to stay at least through the first nights at the Copa. Ava stayed.

On his opening night, Frank was so keyed up that he had to be treated by a doctor before he went on. His throat was bothering him; it had been troubling him for a couple of months, and he seemed absolutely terrified about facing a sophisticated New York club audience. Ava tried to soothe him, without much success, and she sat out front when he came one, her eyes and manner trying to throw him all the support she could. But the crowd wasn't receptive to Frank. For the first time since he'd become a star, Sinatra was confronted by a crowd more interested in talking and joking than listening to him perform. 'Am I speaking too loud for you ladies?' he had to ask, to quiet down one especially noisy group. Later, after a couple of songs, he was forced to plead, 'This is my opening night. Give me a break.'

And then he made the mistake of singing 'Nancy, With the Laughing Face'. The crowd – most of whom probably thought Frank had written the song for his wife, not his daughter – turned toward Ava and began to laugh hysterically at her. She was deeply hurt by Frank's insensitivity, but she brazened it out.

The critical reaction to Sinatra was dreadful, most reviewers writing that his voice had lost its ability to hypnotize. With a severe throat infection and his nerves stretched almost to the breaking point because of the emotional strain – Ava, friends later said, was telling Frank he must file for divorce and marry her, or she would break up the relationship – Frank soon made more headlines by an act that was bizarre even by his standards.

One night Ava, weary of Sinatra's neuroses and his overpowering demands on her, left the Copa after Frank's first show, telling him that she'd wait for him back at their hotel. Instead, she went nightclubbing with friends. The last stop they made was to Bop City, where Ava's second husband, Artie Shaw, was making a comeback.

When he returned to his hotel suite and discovered Ava was not waiting for him as promised, Frank began making phone calls. In a little while he learned Ava was at Bop City, drinking with Shaw and friends. He called her there, 'screaming with jealousy', a friend told reporters. Ava told him there was nothing to be jealous about, the story goes, which made Frank more furious. He told her he was going to kill himself. The threat didn't seem to have much effect on Ava, so Frank pulled out his gun, for which he had a pistol permit, and fired two shots into the mattress. Depending on which gossip is to be believed, Ava either put down the phone as if nothing had happened, or she dropped the phone, screamed, and raced back to the Hampshire House.

In the meantime another resident of the hotel, producer David O. Selznick, had heard the shots from Sinatra's suite and phoned the police. 'I think that son of a bitch Sinatra shot himself', Selznick said. When police and firemen arrived, Frank acted as if they'd all been the victim of a hoax. Police agreed, for they later reported they'd been unable to find any evidence of shots having been fired. That's because the mattress with the bullets had disappeared, apparently exchanged for another one and burned – with the help of police, it was suggested by some who were there.

A couple of days later Ava flew off to London, now equipped with an excuse to get away from Frank: Shooting was due to start any day in Spain on *Pandora and the Flying Dutchman,* a film Ava had signed to do months before. She was relieved to be away from him, the first day or so, but when she settled in her suite in Barcelona her relief turned to an overwhelming loneliness. She and Frank were on the phone constantly, so much that it seemed to be interfering with her acting. But the loneliness didn't last too long. A second-rate Spanish actor and bullfighter, Mario Cabre, who was a first-rate press agent for himself, had been signed to play Ava's lover in the film. He promptly became Ava's lover off-screen as well, although her friends say that for Ava he was simply a minor interlude during a lonely period. Cabre, even worse as a poet, began writing doggeral about his great love for Ava. Naturally, he passed it out to the press, and the headlines said Ava had dropped Frank for a new lover. Ava didn't seem to mind; friends said she was using Cabre to pressure Frank into settling his marital affairs so that they could be married. Frank's reaction was as expected: He began dating Copa showgirls.

A short time later, when he tried to reach a very high note during his Copa show, Frank's voice seemed to break and he appeared to be in pain. But he finished the first show that evening. The physician treating his throat warned Sinatra against doing the next two shows, but Frank went on anyway because he had heard that Lee Mortimer, the Hearst columnist he hated above all other newspapermen, had bet the Copa manager Jack Entratter $100 that he'd never complete his engagement.

Mortimer won his bet. Some time before the third show Frank had suffered a submucosal throat haemorrhage. Stubbornly, he tried to go on despite the pain and the bleeding. Skitch Henderson, his conductor and accompanist at the

Copa, recalled, 'It was tragic and terrifying. Frank opened his mouth to sing after the band introduction and nothing came out. Not a sound. I thought for a fleeting moment that the unexpected pantomime was a joke. But then he caught my eye. I guess the colour drained out of my face as I caught the panic in his. It became so quiet, so intensely quiet in the club. Like they were watching a man walk off a cliff. His face chalk white, Frank gasped something that sounded like "Good night" into the mike and raced off the floor, leaving the audience stunned.'

Ordered to take a complete rest and not to use his voice even for speaking, Frank cancelled the remainder of his engagement. But as reports continued to be printed about Ava's romance with her bullfighter, Frank once more ignored his doctor's warnings and flew to Spain to be with Ava. The press, of course, followed them to restaurants and camped out on their doorstep, demanding to know when they would be married. In Madrid, bullfighter Cabre gave an interview repeating that he and Ava were passionately in love and insisting that as soon as Frank left Spain, he would be romancing the lady again. Sinatra, whose throat was like an open wound, almost had apoplexy. Even when Ava assured him that Cabre was but a joke, Sinatra was not relieved; he decided he had made a terrible mistake chasing after her, that the great publicity his visit to Spain had generated would further effect his declining popularity.

The next morning, as Frank flew back to Los Angeles, Ava and Cabre were back working on the film. But it was the off-set escapades that got the headlines. When their scene was completed, an outdoor scene with hundreds of extras, Cabre kissed her passionately in front of everyone and said, 'Hello baby'. He then bared his chest to the mob and said, 'This is where a bull gored me yesterday. I was distracted by my feeling for Ava. I think of her day and night. She is sublime.' That night he and Ava went to dinner together, then slipped off to be alone. Frank must have read about it in the Hollywood papers the next day.

It seemed to friends that Ava was using Cabre to make Sinatra jealous, that she loved Frank and wanted to marry him, but he wouldn't take that final step of asking for a divorce. Like so many of his women, Ava very early on began to feel that Frank was more completely wrapped up in his children than in his love affair. 'His kids always come first', Ava complained to a friend.

After spending some time with his children, Frank flew off to London where he rented a large flat in Berkeley Square for two months. Ava was already in London doing some interior scenes for her film; she was living in Park Lane, just a few steps from Sinatra. Their reunion, friends reported, was happy and very intense. The relationship was now proceeding so well because English journalists pretty much left them alone.

Frank made his English debut in July of that year, 1950, playing the Palladium with Ava sitting in the centre of the front row to give him support. In contrast to his lukewarm reception on his American dates and his bad record reviews, the English practically swooned over Frank and teenage girls mobbed him as they hadn't done in America for a long while. The reviewer for the *Musical Express* wrote: 'I watched mass hysteria. Was it wonderful? Decidedly so, for this man Sinatra is a superb performer and a great artiste. He had his audience spellbound.' And the man for the *Sunday Chronicle* wrote: 'Bless me, he's *good*! He is as satisfying a one-man performance as the Palladium has ever seen.' During one performance the management was forced to darken the theatre so Frank could escape from an ecstatic crowd of young girls rushing to embrace him. Ava, sitting in her front row seat as usual, was both amused and shocked at their behaviour.

Frank's throat was completely healed, and he loved every moment of the adulation and pandemonium, for it proved he was not a has-been as the American press had begun to hint. Feeling more comfortable in London than in Spain, Hollywood, or New York, because he was treated with respect by the newspapermen who behaved as if his romance with Ava was his own affair and because his old powers of vocal sorcery were working again, Frank once more became the perfect lover and his relationship with Ava was, say friends, as exciting and as beautiful as it had been at the beginning. They accepted invitations to many parties, mingling with aristocracy and royalty. Even Princess Margaret sat at his feet as he sang at a party at the home of a British peer.

In September, while Frank and Ava were back in New York, going to nightclubs and a championship fight, Nancy won a suit for separate maintenance in Santa Monica Superior Court. The property settlement, which Frank signed a week earlier, gave Nancy one-third of his gross earnings on the first $150,000, 10 per cent of the next $150,000, and a declining percentage thereafter, but in no case less than $1,000 a month. Nancy also got the Beverly Hills home, a part-interest in the Sinatra Music Corporation, their Cadillac, furs, jewellery, and custody of the children. Frank kept their house in Palm Springs, two cars, bank accounts, oil interests in Texas, and all rights in musical compositions, recordings, and transcriptions.

Frank also got continuing pressure from Ava to divorce Nancy, for she wouldn't divorce him. Through the rest of that year and into 1951, Frank and Ava were quarrelling constantly. 'Neither of them was very secure in themselves or in their relationship', one of Ava's friends later said of this period. 'They'd been together for a year. Ava wanted marriage. Frank was worried about how his kids would react to a divorce, and about his career which was going downhill fast; Ava's career started shooting to the sky when *Show Boat* was released at this time. And a lot of the arguments came from a basic root – Ava just hated the way Frank handled the press, looking like a goon and getting them all sorts of scandalous headlines. She didn't trust reporters herself, but she would never have attacked them and been nasty to them the way Frank was.'

Finally, in October, 1951, Nancy won a divorce in California, and Frank, urged on by Ava because Nancy's decree would have taken a year to become effective, got a divorce of his own in Nevada. Through all of that year, on each step of the way to the altar, in Mexico, Texas, Spain, and Africa, Frank and Ava were followed by reporters, hounded by them, almost driven wild by them. And he reacted in the usual Sinatra fashion. At Los Angeles International Airport, on their way to a vacation in Mexico, Frank refused to board the plane until all the photographers were removed from the tarmac and the ramp. The photographers refused to be removed and almost started a riot when airport police made attempts to dislodge them. Ava finally made a run for the plane, a magazine over her head; minutes later Frank responded to a plea from the airport staff that the plane couldn't sit there all night and he raced to the plane, knocking cameramen out of his way. In Mexico one of Frank's bodyguards, later identified as a convicted murderer, forced a photographer to surrender his camera after pulling a gun on him and threatening to kill him, then destroyed the film which held shots of Frank and Ava. Another time, Frank nearly drove his car into a group of reporters and photographers at an airport, screaming at one of them, 'Next time I'll kill you, you son-of-a-bitch!' He later apologized to one of them, explaining that he was 'upset' at the time and didn't know his way off the field.

He was more than upset; Frank was close to a nervous breakdown, friends have said. Not only was Nancy continually changing her mind about giving him a divorce, but more dreadful still, Frank's career had gone from a slight dip into a full-scale decline. And Ava had gone from minor actress to international star with the release of *Show Boat* (and, of course, with the constant headlines about her romance with Sinatra).

Frank and Ava were married on 7th November 1951, within a few days after he got his divorce. The wedding, at the Philadelphia home of a wealthy industrialist, was again marred by the press and Frank's reaction to journalists. 'How did those creeps know where we were?' Sinatra shouted as he saw the newsmen camped outside the 'secret' location for the wedding. 'I don't want no circus here!' he continued. 'I'll knock the first guy who tries to get inside on his ass – and I mean it!' In all, however, the ceremony was a quiet one. When it was over, Frank and Ava flew off in a chartered plane for a honeymoon in Havana. They stayed for several days in the Hotel Nacional, which would figure heavily in later charges that Frank was involved with the Mafia.

A fan magazine of the day summed up the Sinatra-Gardner marriage in two headlines. One, just after the wedding, read: NEW NAME FOR HAPPINESS. The other, only four months later, was titled: THE BATTLING SINATRAS.

For the most part, the battles took place because Sinatra was quickly losing his grip on his audiences. A month after their marriage, he and Ava flew off to London where Frank sang at an Anglo-American party sponsored by the Duke of Edinburgh. Appearing on a bill with over a hundred English and American stars, Frank received only polite applause and lukewarm reviews. And it troubled him; a little more than a year after he'd been a sensation in London, he was practically a flop. Only a few months after the London experience, Frank got the first inkling that he was, as the newspapers put it, washed up. He had agreed to appear at the Paramount, the scene of his major triumph, singing from the stage as well as appearing on the screen in his latest film, *Meet Danny Wilson*. At the insistence of his new press agent, Mack Miller, and Ava, that he must take positive steps to mend his relations with the press, Frank flew into New York ten days before his opening at the Paramount to give interviews and pose for photographers. But when he stepped off the plane from Los Angeles, most photographers at the airport ignored his ingratiating and surprising offer to pose for pictures. Frank then sent a note to the Press Photographers' Association: 'I'll always be made up and ready in case you want to shoot any pictures of me.'

He took to visiting radio stations to promote his new record, 'I Hear a Rhapsody', and he began calling reporters to chat and to explain himself. To one he said that about 80 percent of the time he was misquoted and badly treated by the press, but he took the unusual step of admitting he was to blame the rest of the time: 'I lost control of my temper and said things. They were said under great stress and pressure. I'm honestly sorry.' This seemed to be a new Sinatra, attempting to ingratiate himself with the press, a humble and penitent Sinatra who said he owed a lot to reporters and photographers and would be more cooperative in the future.

Writer George Frazier was permitted to interview Sinatra backstage at the Paramount – a highly unusual event in itself – and when he told Frank that the article he would write for *Cosmopolitan* might be less than flattering, Frank winced and stared for a moment in sullen silence. 'Then', Frazier wrote, 'nodding, he became amiable again. "Look", he said "I won't mind if it pans me just as long as it corrects the things I've been doing wrong. . . ." It was the first time', Frazier continued, 'I ever heard him concede that Sinatra is only human . . . For the first time, he seems sceptical of his own infallibility. He no longer takes the view that he is a law unto himself. His sullenness has given way to an authentic eagerness to be pleasant and cooperative . . . In the last year, Frank Sinatra has found a new humility.'

The accuracy of Frazier's assessment can be disputed. As later events show, what Sinatra was demonstrating 'for the first time' *publicly* were the insecurities that had always been hidden beneath the surface; the fear of a loss of artistic power that lurks in the nightmares of every artist; the fear that drove Hemingway to suicide, Fitzgerald to alcohol, and Billy Holliday to heroin.

The structures which had supported Frank's psyche were just then collapsing. His Paramount engagement was disappointing, with empty balconies. Nightclub audiences stopped turning out to see him. Record sales tumbled. And then Columbia tore up his contract, his agency dropped him, his network TV show was cancelled, a film company changed its mind about signing him for a follow-up to *Danny Wilson*. Humility? That was pure press-agentry; inside, Sinatra was hurting. He was suffering through the deepest anguish of his life.

The fact that he had married an actress, a woman with her own career (which was now eclipsing his), added to his anguish. 'The more he slipped, the more he needed Ava to mother him, to give him full-time support', a friend says. 'Ava wasn't about to give up her career, of course, and be the good Italian wife that Frank wanted, and that created a lot of problems between them.' A part of the reason Frank dropped his guard and permitted the insecurities and fears to come through in his talk with George Frazier and with other writers is that Ava was not there to help him cope with his anxieties. In the early months of the year, while Frank was working and agonizing over his Paramount appearance, Ava was asked to play in the film version of Hemingway's *The Snows of Kilimanjaro*; Hemingway himself had told studio chief Darryl Zanuck that Ava should be cast in the role of Cynthia, the Twenties girl loved by the big game hunter in the story. The script was written for Ava by Casey Robinson, who later told Charles Higham that when asked whether she would play the role, 'Ava said, "I'm interested, very interested." She paused and walked away. "But I have a problem, a very great problem. My husband doesn't want me to play it. Frankie's against it." She told me that Frank was so low, his career was so hopeless, that he needed her to go with him to New York, where he had a nightclub engagement. He insisted on it.'

Robinson and the director, Henry King, changed the schedule around and promised Sinatra that Ava's part could be shot in ten days. Sinatra reluctantly consented and Ava began working. Robinson recalled, 'Came the ninth day of shooting. We had only one more sequence to do. Frank kept calling her on the set and making her life pretty darn miserable. I like Frank now, but at the time I hated the little bastard because he was making my girl unhappy. Now I understand him, he was so beaten and insecure. Then came the last scene, the scene on the battlefield in Spain when Ava is dying. There was a problem – we had a great many extras, four or five hundred in all, and to satisfy the ten-day agreement we'd have to shoot into the night, which would have been horribly expensive. We decided to go over the ten days and break the agreement. When King and I told Ava, all hell broke loose. She became hysterical. She called New York and Frank was furious with her. God knows how we got through the last day.'

Ava made it to New York in time for Frank's Paramount opening, but the disastrous audience reception and cutting newspaper stories about the loss of his fans angered him and he took most of that anger out on Ava. Though so much alike, their temperaments clashed because each seemed to be withholding a part of themselves from the other, getting rid of hostilities by constant bickering and occasional violent fights but not getting to the root of their problems, unable to face up to them. Ava said of Frank during this period, 'He has a fine old Sicilian temper that explodes as often as mine, and he has an irritating habit of walking out of the room in the middle of an argument, leaving me burning inside.' And Ava, beset by her own fears and anxieties, could not permit Frank to come as close as a lover should be able. Ava's friends and former lovers have all remarked on this withdrawal.

Italian actor Walter Chiari, one of Ava's first lovers after her marriage to Sinatra broke up, years later told Charles Higham, 'I don't believe she ever totally and committedly loved me as I loved her . . . Somehow when we were together I often felt I was alone, that she had withdrawn from me in some mysterious and unsettling way . . . I had the nagging feeling I could never possess her. The only one who "possessed" Ava Gardner was that adorable Ava herself.'

And a woman friend said of Ava's affair with Howard Hughes, a few years before she met Frank, 'Her essential remoteness, that "hollow feeling" at the heart of the relationship, drove Hughes crazy, just as it did Mickey Rooney, her first husband.'

That 'hollow feeling' also disturbed Sinatra, an intuitive and sensitive man who could not understand why the woman he loved, and who said she loved him, held back an important part of herself; at the same time, a part of his own self was hidden away from her and she must also have realized it. Apparently unable to understand it, however, Ava began to grow resentful of all the hours he spent with his ex-wife and the attention he lavished on his children. 'She was', a friend says, 'dreadfully afraid Frank would leave her and go back to Nancy, because of the kids. That's how insecure that woman was. And Frank – well, he was still jealous about Rooney and Shaw and Howard Hughes, anyone Ava had ever slept with or been rumoured to have slept with. They were a couple of super-stars as immature as adolescents with acne.' But Frank was in such precarious emotional shape, he said in an interview at that time, he began seeing a New York psychiatrist.

In May, back in Hollywood after the Paramount disaster, Ava was rushed to Cedars of Lebanon Hospital after attending Frank's performance at the Cocoanut Grove. She underwent surgery and the facts of her illness were kept secret. Some friends said she'd suffered a miscarriage; others said she'd had another abortion – her first, while she was dating actor Howard Duff steadily, was performed by a butcher and Ava was later told she would probably never be able to hold a foetus for nine months.

The summer was relatively quiet for the Sinatras, so far as raucous headlines went. Ava flew off to Utah to do a film and was so deeply depressed by the heat of the desert sun and the flies that she called Frank in desperation and asked him to join her. He immediately flew in and stayed for two weeks, trying to bring her out of a foul mood – one that was made much fouler, incidentally, because she despised the director on the film, because he used to fly to Los Angeles on Friday night, fly back the next morning with a plane-load of call girls to carouse and fornicate with through the week-end, then curse out everyone on the set on Monday mornings through his monstrous hangover.

Ava got through that experience with Frank's help and an important assignment from MGM: to play opposite Clark Gable in a remake of the film he'd made with Jean Harlow years before, *Red Dust*. The new movie, called *Mogambo*, would be filmed in Africa. Frank was upset, at first, that Ava would be leaving him for an extended period; then he juggled his schedule so that he'd be free to accompany her.

Though he was still seriously troubled that his mass audience was gone, Frank had a personal boost in the last months of 1952 as he began to perceive that he was now reaching an older and more sophisticated crowd, the night-club audiences. His Cocoanut Grove reception had been the warmest in a year, but that could have been because it was a Hollywood audience, composed of many friends and members of his clan. He had been well received at the Desert Inn in Las Vegas in August. And at the Riviera in Fort Lee, New Jersey, where Frank opened in September, the audiences were enthusiastic and the reviews were better than they had been in many months. *Variety*, for example, said that Sinatra displayed a lot of 'self-assurance and a knowing way with a crowd, whatever the misadventures of his personal life and career'.

Within a few hours of that review, back into the headlines came Frankie with another misadventure. Ava was attending the premier of *Kilimanjaro* in New York. Frank couldn't be at the theatre with her because of his Riviera schedule, but between shows he was driven at breakneck speed into Manhattan, where he found Ava and brought her back to the Riviera for the late show of the evening. The place was packed, and most of the audience stood up to gawk as Ava was escorted to a front table. Her eyes had barely grown accustomed to the dark in the swank club when Frank came on and the lights on him illuminated another stage-side table, at which sat Marilyn Maxwell, for whom Frank almost broke up his marriage several years before. Ava was angry and the anger turned to rage when she thought she detected in Frank, during the singing of an especially tender love ballad, certain subtle seductive gestures aimed at Maxwell. In the middle of the song, Ava got up and stalked out, cursing all the way. She grabbed the next available plane back to Hollywood. The moment she got home, she changed their unlisted number so Frank couldn't phone her. The next word Frank received from Ava was a bitter note wrapped around her wedding ring.

'They were both so jealous', a friend says, 'and they were constantly playing on one another's jealousy. Like little kids standing there, punching one another until they both gave up. Except, neither Ava nor Frank had enough sense to stop punching.'

They were reconciled, eventually, after Frank publicly let it be known he desperately wanted his wife back, and after friends told Ava that Frank appeared on the verge of a breakdown and was talking about the futility of his life. But it didn't last long. Less than a week after their head-lined reconciliation, Frank threw some clothes into a duffle bag and moved into songwriter Jimmy Van Heusen's house.

This explosion involved another one of Frank's old loves, Lana Turner, who had become a close friend of Ava. There are several versions of what caused the fight, but the most credible is this: Ava had given a week-end party at Frank's Palm Springs home before they were to fly off together for Africa and the filming of *Mogambo*. One night Frank and all the week-end guests, except Lana, left the house to go to another party. Ava also stayed behind. Frank returned un-expectedly and, depending on which gossip you consult, either found Ava and Lana in bed together or found them sitting around drinking and comparing Frank's sexual prowess to Artie Shaw's, to whom both Ava and Lana had been married. The latter version is probably the truth since Frank was terribly jealous of Shaw and believed Ava was still fascinated by the musician and since, most of all, Sinatra's Sicilian mentality would never have permitted him to con-tinue loving a woman who swung both ways. In any case, Frank flew into a rage and ordered the two women out of the house. Ava refused and the argument grew so violent that neighbours called police.

Frank moved in with Van Heusen, cancelled his plans to fly to Africa, then had a change of heart after hearing that Ava was dating another man. Frank once more let it be known through newspaper interviews that he wanted Ava back. His two public pleas to Ava to take him back were so uncharacteristic of the man that it was obvious to everyone Frank had grown absolutely dependent on Ava. It was the first time in his life, since leaving Hoboken, that he appeared to depend on anyone but himself. They were reconciled again at a rally in Las Vegas for Democratic presidential candidate Adlai Stevenson. A few days later they flew to North Carolina to visit Ava's family, then they went to Kenya.

Before leaving for Africa, Frank read James Jones's novel,

From Here to Eternity and immediately began badgering executives at Columbia, which had bought the film rights, to give him the role of Private Maggio. 'For the first time in my life I was reading something I really had to do', Frank later said about his obsessive drive to get the role. 'I just felt it, I just knew I could do it, and I just couldn't get it out of my head . . . I knew that if a picture was ever made, I was the only actor to play Maggio, the funny and sour Italo-American. I knew Maggio. I went to high school with him in Hoboken. I was beaten up with him. I might have *been* Maggio.' He mounted an enormous campaign to get the part. He sent Ava to see the late Harry Cohn, King Cohn, known as the biggest bastard in Hollywood and proud of his reputation. Cohn was unreceptive to her. So Ava went to see Cohn's wife, Joan, and asked 'me to intercede with Harry to give Frank the part'. Frank Costello, the New York Mafia leader, told his Copacabana dinner friends that he was asked to intercede for Sinatra; he had known Sinatra through Willie Moretti, Costello said, and while he and Frank weren't close friends they had met on many occasions over the years. So when Frank asked for his help, how could Costello refuse? He, of course, got Frank the role. That seems to be a bit of Mafia bragging, however. Others, closer to Costello, say that Sinatra never personally approached the *mafioso* for help. Costello simply read in the papers that Sinatra wanted the role, for Frank was telling everyone, including columnists, that he would play Maggio for nothing. Costello then called several West Coast Mafia men who control film industry unions and asked them to intercede for Sinatra. Cohn ignored them.

Desperate because he was leaving for Africa with Ava and was afraid he would lose the part, Frank went to see Cohn himself, almost begging for the role.

'Shit, Frank', Cohn reportedly said. 'Maggio is an *actor's* part. You're a *singer*, not an actor. We want an *actor*.'

Frank went on and on, telling Cohn he *was* Maggio, that no actor in the world understood the soldier's character as Frank understood it, insisting that a singer is acting every moment he's out there in front of an audience. Cohn didn't buy any of the dozens of arguments Frank threw at him. After a while, Frank decided to play his last card. Knowing that Cohn was a miser when it came to paying actors, Frank asked, 'About the money?'

'Who mentioned money?' Cohn shot back. 'But what about the money?'

'I get a hundred-fifty thousand a film. . . .'

'You *used* to get a hundred-fifty. Not any more.'

'Right, I used to get it. I don't want anything near that much.'

'I'm not buying at any price', Cohn said. 'But just for the record, what's your price?'

'I'll play Maggio for a thousand a week.'

'You want it that bad?' Cohn said.

Sinatra started to say again that it was written for him and no one else, but Cohn interrupted: 'We'll see, Frank. But I have some other actors – *real* actors – to test first.' Sinatra had better sense than to get angry at that last put-down, at any of Cohn's rather sadistic thrusts, and he held his tongue. He was feeling totally depressed. The part, he was certain, would be given to someone else; Cohn reportedly made it clear that Eli Wallach would be best for the role.

And then the man originally scheduled to produce the film for Columbia, Sylvan Simon, died. Buddy Adler, who had known Sinatra for some years, was given the assignment. Frank went to see him, to plead for a screen test. He called Adler almost every day. Adler said it was basically up to King Cohn, but he'd try to convince him to authorize the test. 'I'll play the damn part for $50 a week', Frank said at one point, according to Adler.

When he flew off to Africa with Ava, Frank was in absolute misery because he was certain he'd never even get a screen test. Once in Nairobi, he became alternately sullen and explosive; the distance from Hollywood seemed to guarantee he'd never get the part, yet he couldn't leave because of his jealousy. They quarrelled constantly, wouldn't speak to one another for days, then quarrelled again. Contributing to Frank's dark mood was the fact that Ava was the star of one of the year's biggest films and he couldn't even get a lousy screen test.

Adler's cable finally came, inviting him to appear for a screen test. Still playing the role of bastard, Cohn made certain there was no offer to pay for the 27,000-mile flight back to Hollywood. Frank boarded the next plane.

Buddy Adler later said, 'He surprised us by appearing in Hollywood thirty-six hours after my cable. I was a little startled when I gave him the script of the drunk scene and he handed it back, saying, "I don't need this. I've read it many times." I didn't think he had a chance anyway, so I said, "Well, okay." Since his was the last test of the day, I didn't intend going down on the stage. But I got a call from the director, Fred Zinnemann. "You'd better come down here", he said. "You'll see something unbelievable. I already have it in the camera. I'm not using film this time. But I want you to see it."

'Frank thought he was making another take – and he was terrific. I thought to myself, if he's like that in the movie it's a sure Academy Award. But we had to have Harry Cohn's okay on casting and he was out of town. So Frank went back to Africa.'

Apparently neither Zinnemann nor Adler were gracious enough to tell Frank how marvellous he'd been, even after making him work through a retake with no film in the cameras. Frank knew his acting had been superb; he felt it inside himself and he knew it from the reaction of everyone on the sound stage. He was exultant when he returned to Nairobi, loaded down with Christmas gifts for Ava (which he bought with money borrowed from a friend). He even led a group of Kenyans singing carols on Christmas Eve, which was also Ava's birthday. Not even the 'miscarriage' Ava suffered while Frank was in Hollywood dampened his spirits. (That miscarriage was actually an abortion, says the cameraman on the film, Robert Surtees. 'Ava hated Frank so intensely at this stage, she couldn't stand the idea of having his baby', Surtees told Charles Higham. 'She went to London to have an abortion. I know because my wife went to London to be at her side at all times through the operation and afterwards, and to bring her back on the plane. She told my wife, "I hated Frankie so much. I wanted that baby to go unborn." ')

As the days went by and there was no word from Hollywood, not even a private communication from director or producer to bolster Frank's spirits, he became bitter and sullen again, and he and Ava once more began quarrelling. Then a cable arrived informing him he'd been given the role, but at only a thousand dollars a week; Frank had meant it when he said he'd play the part for nothing and he wired back his acceptance. Pacing up and down in Ava's tent on location, the cable clutched in his hands, Frank said over and over again, 'Now I'll show the bastards.'

Cohn's widow, now Joan Cohn Harvey, recalls how Sinatra was finally chosen : 'The part of Maggio was really only considered for two people, Frank and Eli Wallach. Harry used to work very late right here in this bedroom-office. They were all gathered here late one night – Harry, the producer, the director, everyone else involved – arguing about who should be Maggio. Finally, Harry asked me to go down to our projection room and have a look at the tests. It was the scene where Maggio gets drunk outside the barracks. Well, Eli Wallach is a terrific actor, but I thought he was too Jewish for Maggio, not Italian enough. I thought it *had* to be Frank, so I went upstairs and told them so. Harry turned to the others. "You see", he said, "That's what I've been trying to tell you." '

If her version is correct and not just a widow's attempt to make her husband look less the bastard, then Cohn either believed Sinatra was perfect for the role from the beginning – which makes his treatment of Frank even less excusable – or he was as overwhelmed as every one now claims to have been by the screen test.

A week after getting the cable, Frank flew back to Hollywood to get ready for the filming of *Eternity* and to try and rebuild his broken career. He signed on with the William Morris office, which began hunting for another record company. Manie Sachs, one of Frank's closest friends, had left his executive position at Columbia and gone over to RCA Victor, but he was unable to convince his colleagues there to sign Frank to a contract. Finally, the young and aggressive Capitol Records offered Frank a one-year contract – no advance, and all recording costs were to be borne by Frank. Sinatra signed, and in the seven years with Capitol he turned out some of the best recordings of his life.

But it was *Eternity* to which he devoted most of his energies, because he knew he would show the bastards – not only King Cohn, but the reporters, the fans, and everyone who had knifed him when he'd begun to slip.

'Frank dreamt, slept, and ate his part', producer Buddy Adler said after the filming of *Eternity* in March and April, 1953. 'He has the most amazing sense of timing and occasionally he'll drop in a word or two that makes the line actually bounce. It's just right. He never made a fluff. And this from a fellow who never really had any training.'

'He played Maggio so spontaneously', director Fred Zinnemann said, 'We almost never had to reshoot a scene.'

Frank so completely identified with his role that members of the crew unconsciously began calling him 'Maggio'. As he had said, he did *know* Maggio. So much so that Sinatra practically began directing his own scenes himself. Cohn's widow recalls, 'One night, when we were shooting in Hawaii, Harry and I were having dinner in the Royal Hawaiian when Harry had a hysterical call from Buddy Adler, complaining that Frank wouldn't do a scene the way Zinnemann wanted him to. Harry went straight over and calmed things down. He told Frank to do it Fred's way first, then his own way, and then they'd decide when they were cutting it whose way was best. Which they did. Frank's version stayed. That happened quite often during shooting and Frank was almost always right.'

She added, 'Frank really knew Maggio, he lived him. Long after the film was gone and forgotten he would send telegrams from all over Europe signed, "Maggio".'

A change seemed to come over Frank even before the film was completed. As Maggio, he was the insecure, beaten underdog, a character he had claimed would have been his had he not become a rich and famous singer. But though he is said to have lived the part of Maggio, there was clearly something else going on inside him. Even while working on the film, Frank Sinatra knew it would bring him to the top of his profession again and he began to behave as if he were already there.

By the time the filming was completed, Frank was the old Sinatra, a swagger in his walk, his head held high, 'a don't-give-a-damn guy', as Joan Cohn Harvey put it. 'I gave a dinner party in Honolulu at the end of shooting, for the cast and some of the Army brass who had been helping us with the film', she said. 'Frank was sitting on my right and on his right was the wife of the commanding general. Frank was getting a bit loud and his language wasn't too hot, so I leaned over and whispered, "Frank, that's the general's wife beside you." And Frank shouted very loudly, "Fuck the general's wife!" '

Early in May, after filming ended, Frank began a three-month concert tour of Europe. Ava went with him. By then the entire film industry had learned that something marvellous had taken place in Hawaii, that Frank Sinatra had given one of the finest performances ever seen on the screen, that he would be the King again. The people who had ignored him during his pursuit of Ava, the black headlines, and the career-slide now began sucking up to him again as if he were indeed *Il Padrone*. Further, Sinatra began to feel confident in the recording studio again. Nelson Riddle, a former trombonist with Tommy Dorsey and the most sought-after arranger-composer-conductor on the West Coast in 1953, was now producing Frank's records for Capitol. Riddle brought to Frank's records, starting with 'My One and Only Love', which was laid on tape a week before Frank went to Europe with Ava, the swinging sound that carried Frank beyond the belting of the Frankie Laines into a new territory of which he became the master – the near-jazz sound of brassy, driving swing, counterpointed by flowing strings.

He was on the way up again and he knew it, and it destroyed his relationship with Ava. 'When he was down and out', she said after the European tour, 'he was so sweet. But now that he's gotten successful again he's become his old arrogant self. We were happy when he was on the skids.'

Perhaps Ava was happy when Frank was down, but his happiness depended on his being up again; Ava seemed to react against Frank the more his career improved. At times she seemed to be getting some kind of revenge on him. She had just completed the major shooting on *Knights of the Round Table* in England and Ireland, Frank with her much of the time after his highly successful European tour ended. Since Ava had only a few small scenes to shoot in London and had almost a week off before she was needed again, Frank asked her to accompany him back to America where he was due to open at the 500 Club in Atlantic City. She said she'd rather go to Spain for a rest. Frank, never able to forget her affair with the actor-bullfighter, grew furious. The argument was so loud that other tenants of the building in which they had a flat called the management. Frank stormed out of the apartment. He returned a few hours later and discovered Ava had left and locked him out. Still later, he learned that Ava had gone to a Piccadilly club to see Walter Chiari, who did a burlesque of Frank while Ava sat at ringside, breaking up with laughter and encouraging Chiari to greater heights of comedy by shouting, 'That's just like Frank! It's so funny! More! More!'

Frank flew back to New York on 12th August. Even the reviews of *Eternity*, which was released a few days earlier, didn't cheer him up too much despite the prediction of most critics that Frank would get an Academy Award nomination and probably the Oscar itself. But Frank slowly came out of his funk, especially after it became clear he was now so much in demand that he was offered $6,000 to help launch the new 'Milton Berle Show', receiving almost as much for one evening's work on TV as he had been paid for eight weeks on *Eternity*.

On 2nd September, two days before Frank was due to open an engagement at the Riviera, Ava flew into New York. She had not cabled him about her arrival and he didn't meet her at the airport, which infuriated her. She took a suite at the Hampshire House, while Frank fumed at the Waldorf.

Neither would phone the other. The night he opened at the Riviera, Ava went to a Broadway premier. Frank was a smash hit, packing them in and amazing the reviewers by 'giving one of the greatest performances of his career', as one critic wrote.

Frank's mother, Dolly, effected a reconciliation a couple of days later, getting them together at her home. It lasted only a month. Ava had gone to their Palm Springs home to rest – friends said that now *she* was near a nervous breakdown – and Frank went to Las Vegas to fulfill a nightclub commitment. Late in October her studio announced that the Sinatras had decided to end their two-year marriage.

Ava complained to friends and to several columnists that Sinatra had become overbearing, too demanding, and didn't really give a damn about her. 'Frank doesn't love me. He would rather go out with some other girl, any other girl', she told one writer. She told another that Frank's cronies were constantly around, making it impossible for them to be alone together. For example, she said, a couple of nights after the reconciliation at Dolly's, Frank left her in their Hampshire House suite to go to the Riviera, asking her to wait up for him. But instead of returning to her at the end of his performance, he went to a restaurant with his friends and stayed there until closing at four a.m. When he did get back to their suite, Ava said, she asked him whether it wasn't a little late and he snapped, 'Don't cut the corners too close on me, baby. This is the way my life is going to be from now on.' And he meant it, she said. When she tried to be alone with him at Palm Springs, during still another brief reconciliation, she found that Frank had invited several of his buddies as house guests. As the intimacy she wanted evaporated and she complained to Frank about it, he loudly defended his right to have his friends around him.

And so it went for months, Sinatra loudly proclaiming that he and Ava would get together again and Ava saying it was over for good. After Frank finally admitted to reporters that his marriage was over, he again came close to collapse. Weak, undernourished, and rundown by the stress of the collapse of his marriage, Sinatra checked into Mt. Sinai

Hospital in New York for a series of tests and a complete rest, amid rumours – untrue – that he had attempted suicide.

A friend of Sinatra in that period says today, 'They were playing a strange kind of game with each other. Ava was so insecure and so close to collapse at this time that she had to have proof positive that Frank loved her. So she put him through some strange tests. Professionally difficult tests, as if she wanted him to prove that she was more important than his career, which was just then taking off the ground again. For instance, take the big and final battle, when they were in London together and she locked him out. Frank had the big club engagement back in the States, but Ava insisted that he wait for her to complete a few weeks work in London, then they'd return together. But Frank couldn't; he had to come back at least a couple of weeks before the opening to get ready. There were rehearsals, he needed a few new songs, which meant working with arrangers, and all the thousands of details that go into a professional performance. Ava wouldn't listen; she demanded that he wait around in London, expecting him to shove two weeks of rehearsal into two days. So, to get even, Ava didn't tell him when she was flying back to New York. Then, to show her independence or something, she wouldn't attend his opening. And Frank – well he was the old Sinatra, holding court with his buddies, making it with a lot of women, doing that whole Sicilian thing he's so noted for.'

Joan Cohn Harvey adds another element to that final split. 'Ava told me she'd had an affair with a bullfighter in Spain and was going to tell Frank all about it. I told her she was crazy and suggested that even if he found out she should deny everything (as she had done in the past) but she told him anyway and, of course, that was the end of it.'

Still another facet of the troubles between Frank and Ava was cited by the late Jimmy Cannon, who was Sinatra's favourite sports columnist and was close to Frank during this period. Cannon once told me, 'The trouble with Frank's relationship with Ava was that he couldn't do anything for her. She was on top. And I think he learned that when a man is down, especially a man as proud as Frank is, a woman can't really do anything to help him. If the woman's on top, a man like Frank just hurts. Her career gets in the way of his needs, because a man like Frank needs a woman around him twenty-four hours a day. Or whenever he wants her to be around. Ava couldn't buy that. And then, when he got his strength back, professionally and down inside himself, his needs changed. Sure, he still loved her. But he was the King again, and he wanted to be around with his buddies to show it and have fun with it. And that's when a woman gets in the way.'

Over the next few months Frank and Ava attempted to reconcile a couple of times, but by then she had grown tired of him and his intensity and demands on her. 'Frank wanted her to come home with him from Madrid, where she went to live', a friend says, 'but she refused. She had *The Barefoot Contessa* to do, and she wasn't about to destroy her career to play the role of Frank's mother, which is what he seemed to want.' So Ava turned to a new bullfighter, Dominguin, and Sinatra turned to Oscar for support.

'The greatest change in my life came the night they gave me the Oscar', he said a short time after winning his Academy Award in March, 1954. 'It's funny about that statue. You walk up on that stage as if you are in a dream and they hand you that little man before twenty or thirty million people and you have to fight to keep the tears back. It's a moment. Like your first girl or your first kiss. Like the first time you hit a guy and he went down. I've heard actors kid about the Academy Awards. Don't believe them. It was a big moment in their lives.'

It was, by far, the biggest moment in Sinatra's life; the biggest and most dramatic comeback in Hollywood's brief history. At a party after the awards Frank was once more his wise-cracking, cocky old self, obviously glowing over his personal triumph. But later, in the bachelor apartment Frank shared with Jule Styne, the mask slipped again. Styne (who had moved in on Frank's insistence because a woman Styne loved deeply had left him and Frank was worried about him) later told a writer what Frank was like in that period immediately after his marriage to Ava failed.

'I come home at night and enter the living room and it's like a funeral parlour', Styne said. 'The lights are dim and they just about light up several pictures of Ava. Frank sits in front of them with a bottle of brandy. After I get into bed, I can hear him pacing back and forth. It goes on for hours. At four a.m., I awake to hear him dialling someone on the phone. It's his first wife, Nancy. I hear him say, "You're the only one who understands me." After he hangs up he starts pacing again. He seldom falls asleep until the sun is high in the sky.'

Another of Sinatra's friends from that period recalled, 'One time he called us over to play cards. When we got there we found he had just been on the telephone to his first wife, Nancy. Sometimes he needs advice or wants somebody to talk to or maybe he's just lonely, so he calls Nancy. Well, this time she was mad at him. She wouldn't talk to him.

'By the time we got the game started he didn't even want to play any more. He went into the den, opened a bottle, and started drinking alone. So we keep the game going a while, then Sammy Cahn gets up and he goes in to try to get Frank to join us. So what does he see?

There's Frank drinking a toast to a picture of Ava with a tear running down his face. So Sammy comes back and we start playing again. All of a sudden we hear a crash. We all get up and we run into the den and there's Frank. He had taken the picture of Ava, frame and all, and thrown it down. Then he had picked up the picture, ripped it into little pieces and thrown it on the floor.

'So we all tell him, "Come on, Frank, you got to forget all about that. Come and play some cards with us." So he says, "I'm through with her. I never want to see her again. I'm all right. I've just been drinking too much." So we go back to the game and a little while later Sammy goes back to Frank and there he is on his hands and knees picking up the torn pieces of the picture and trying to put it back together again. Well, he gets all the pieces together except the one for the nose. He becomes frantic looking for it, and we all get down on our hands and knees and try to help him.

All of a sudden the door bell rings. It's a delivery boy with more liquor. So Frank goes to the back door to let him in, but when he opens it, the missing piece flutters out of his sleeve or something. Well, Frank is so happy he takes off his gold watch and gives it to the delivery boy.'

Over the next couple of years Sinatra tried numerous times to get Ava back, apparently on his own terms, but Ava wouldn't bend; friends say she was still in love with him but wanted him back on her terms – on his knees, penitent. She had set up residence in Nevada for the divorce, but never bothered to pick up the papers. Publicly she said the marriage was over, but privately she told friends she was seeing a psychiatrist, hoping to work out her problems so that she could learn to live with Frank.

His own attempts to win her back appeared rather strange to their friends. He took young actresses to various Hollywood and Vegas nightspots, quite obviously holding their hands and kissing them. He began to date Gloria Vanderbilt. He seemed to think he could make Ava so jealous she'd take him back, the gossips said.

But Frank's career was zooming and he put all his efforts into work. His recordings for Capitol were selling as the Sinatra of old used to sell. Nightclub appearances were bringing him $50,000 a week. In his film, *Suddenly,* the first made after *Eternity,* Sinatra won superb reviews for the 'spine-chilling reality' of his acting in the role of a presidential assassin. His next film, *Not as a Stranger,* brought him even greater critical acclaim. 'Man, I feel eight feet tall', he said late in 1955. 'Everything is ahead of me. I'm on top of the world. I'm buoyant.'

His buoyancy was for public consumption, however. Friends said publicly that he still loved Ava. And he didn't get angry at those friends who talked about his private feelings, because he was once more using newspaper columnists to get the word to Ava that he still cared. She didn't seem to care, however.

For a while, in the spring of 1956, it appeared as though they might get together again. Ava was living in a villa she had bought in Madrid, and Frank was scheduled to go to

Spain to film *The Pride and the Passion*. Ava laughed when friends suggested the possibility of a reconciliation, yet her mood seemed to be one of electric anticipation at his arrival, and she called in a crew of Spanish women to help her do over the house 'as if she were getting a honeymoon cottage ready', one friend told a columnist.

But Frank got his revenge. Instead of coming to Madrid alone he brought with him a Hollywood starlet, Peggy Connolly, whom he had been dating for a couple of months. Ava was furious. She told friends what she thought of Frank, and when she ran into him in restaurants, she pretended he wasn't there.

By this time, Sinatra was soaring high: His films were box-office smashes, and he was recording almost constantly, turning out some of the finest records of his career (and some dreadful ones because 'he'd rather be out playing with his buddies', as one of his producers put it); *Metronome* and other music magazines once again selected him as the best singer; he packed them in once more at the New York Paramount; and he had captured and captivated his most vital audience, the big-money saloon crowd.

His new-found authority and popularity was made clear, as it always is in Western society, by the amount of money he was able to command for his services – three million dollars from the ABC-TV network for twenty-six half-hour shows and two hour-long specials, with Frank in full control over what would appear on the screen. But although his first broadcast, in October, 1957, attracted a large audience, the ratings soon began to fall off. Even the Christmas show, with Bing Crosby as a special guest, was a failure. At first no one involved in the production could understand what was wrong, but after a time it became apparent: the 'real' Sinatra was missing. The public Sinatra, the man of arrogance and sexuality, the headline-maker, the controversial Sinatra, was replaced on the TV screen by a man displaying a studied unconcern, a nice man inviting the audience into his living room to share some fun with him and his friends. The public was more entertained by what Sinatra was doing off-screen than by what he was doing on the box and it stopped watching the box.

The off-screen entertainment was indeed more titillating. Frank had been dating Lauren Bacall after Humphrey Bogart's death from cancer in January, 1957. Frank and Bogey had been close friends; both were iconoclasts who hated the Hollywood phonies. A couple of months after Bogey died, Frank began dating Bacall in an attempt to pull her out of her widow's depression. Almost immediately, the gossip columnists began reporting that a serious romance was developing and that it could end up in marriage. There seems to have been some truth to the rumours, according to friends of both, but Sinatra and Bacall were much too aware of what havoc international publicity could do to their relationship, and they tried to be as discreet as possible. The gossip mills churned even further in June, when Ava Gardner finally filed for a Mexican divorce. It was granted on 5th July, at the very moment that Sinatra was sailing in the Pacific on a chartered 102-foot yacht with a group of close friends, including Lauren Bacall.

The relationship with Bacall grew warmer through the year and into the following March, and then suddenly ended. A Hollywood gossip columnist, Louella Parsons, encountering Bacall at a party given by Zsa Zsa Gabor, bluntly asked about marriage. Lauren replied, 'Why don't you ask Frank?' Louella promised she would call Sinatra in Florida, where he was fulfilling an engagement, and put the question to him, apparently believing Lauren herself was trying to learn where she stood. But then Lauren's escort at the party, literary agent I. P. Lazar, pulled the columnist aside and said, 'Don't you dare say I told you this, but since you know anyway, yes, they're going to get married. It's true.'

Louella broke the story the next day and Bacall immediately learned where she stood – Sinatra cut her dead.

But the columnists insisted on matching Frank with someone, anyone. After breaking up with Bacall, he went off to Monte Carlo for the premiere of his film, *Kings Go Forth*, a $50-a-person invitational gala for the benefit of Princess Grace's favourite charity, the UN Refugee Fund. Sinatra stopped off in London for some club-hopping with Peter Lawford, and immediately the columnists speculated that he was going to marry American-born Lady Beatty, whom he had dated rather steadily for a time. And when Sinatra announced he was negotiating with one of Brigitte Bardot's producers to do a film with her, newspaper writers said he was romancing the actress.

All the writers missed the one big Sinatra romance that would have been more sensational than even his pursuit of Ava Gardner. It was around this time, early 1959, that Frank Sinatra and Marilyn Monroe became lovers. Marilyn's marriage to playwright Arthur Miller was breaking up at the time and she turned to Sinatra for support.

'Frank has always been so kind and understanding', Marilyn told friends some months before her death in the summer of 1962. 'When I'm with him I don't feel I have to take pills or see a psychiatrist or anything else. He makes me feel secure and happy. He makes me laugh. I think he is the only man who has taught me how to live life. And he's really a gentleman.'

Her need for Sinatra seemed rather strange to her friends because there was a time that Marilyn despised him for participating in a rather ungentlemanly act. That was the famous 'wrong door' raid in 1954, when Marilyn was in the process of divorcing Joe DiMaggio. Sinatra and DiMaggio were friends at the time. Not willing to accept the fact that Marilyn was actually breaking up their marriage, trying desperately to hold on to her, DiMaggio asked Sinatra's help. He wanted to catch his wife in a compromising situation, not for evidence against her in a divorce action, but as a club he could use to persuade her to return to him.

Sinatra reportedly asked one of his New York friends to hire a private investigator to begin following Marilyn. On a November night in 1954 the sleuth tailed her to an apartment where she was visiting a girlfriend and then called DiMaggio. He called Sinatra. Both rushed over to the small apartment building where Marilyn was visiting. DiMaggio, apparently believing he'd find Marilyn in a lesbian relationship and that evidence of this, most of all, would be a strong weapon to force her to remain married to him, ordered the apartment raided.

The private detective, Barney Ruditsky, joined by another clown who called himself an investigator, plus a couple of other men including a photographer, rushed into the building; Sinatra, by all accounts, remained outside in his car. The raiding party broke down the door of an apartment and snapped a couple of quick photos of a woman who was shocked out of a deep sleep and who became hysterical at seeing the flashbulbs and the dim figures of strange men in her bedroom. Someone turned on a light. Someone else shouted, 'We've got the wrong place!' And they all turned and fled, leaving the woman behind in a state of panic. (The woman whose apartment had been broken into sued DiMaggio and Sinatra for $200,000 after a scandal magazine broke the story a couple of years later and a California investigatory agency looked into the matter. The suit was quietly settled out of court.)

Although Marilyn was furious at Sinatra and DiMaggio when she learned of the raid, she later forgave them both. She came to understand how deeply DiMaggio loved her; she felt Sinatra had gone along on the raid not only to bolster a friend who was in deep emotional turmoil but also to exact a bit of revenge – she had walked out on the film *Pink Tights*, which she was supposed to have made with Sinatra; and he was still angry about that at the time of her problems with DiMaggio.

Years later, when Frank and Marilyn had become lovers, she could laugh about the raid. She told one friend, 'I don't know if Frank will ever live that one down.'

Although the press didn't learn about the Sinatra-Monroe romance until at least a year after it began, close friends knew and they say it was so serious the couple had even discussed marriage. But Marilyn said it could never happen. 'We don't really have that much to offer each other as man and wife', she told several intimates. 'We're both famous, we're both at the top of our professions and we both have enough money to last a long time. The needs are missing.

Besides, I have to reach beyond Hollywood for what I want in the future.

'Also', she added, 'marriage could never happen because I think Frank is still in love with Nancy Senior and will go back to her some day.'

But then, perversely, Sinatra announced he was going to marry dancer Juliet Prowse. When Marilyn learned about the marriage plans, she later told friends, she went over to her neighbour's house on Doheny Drive – the neighbour was Gloria Lovell, Sinatra's secretary – and they sat up together all night crying because they thought Frank was making a serious mistake.

Some friends of Sinatra still question whether his 'engagement' to Juliet wasn't all part of the revenge he was getting on another dancer, Barrie Chase, who had walked out on the film *Can Can*. When Sinatra heard Barrie had quit the film, he reportedly shouted, 'How could she do this to me? Doesn't she know *I'm* in the picture? I'll tell you what I'm going to do. Whoever they get to replace her, I'll make her *known*.'

Juliet was the replacement. By the end of filming, Sinatra was dating her steadily and telling the gossip columnists about their relationship; he called reporters to inform them he thought she had an enormous talent; he booked her on his TV special and made a point of telling his forty million viewers he thought she was a very special kind of girl.

A year later, after dating a number of other women while continuing to promote Juliet, Sinatra gave her an engagement ring and the largest headlines of her life. A few weeks went by, and then Sinatra announced the engagement was off 'because of career conflicts'. Snapped a friend, 'Talk about short engagements; Frank has had longer engagements in Las Vegas.' Most of Sinatra's friends at the time believed, and still believe, the marriage plans were designed solely to boost Juliet's career– 'doing the kid a favour', as it was said in the Clan.

Yet that doesn't quite ring true. It wasn't necessary for Frank to have gone so far as to announce wedding plans, to meet Juliet's parents, and presumably to receive their blessings, simply to promote her career. It seems plain that Frank did want to marry her, but on his own terms. Those terms were, as they've always been, that his woman's career must take second place to his special needs. During their brief engagement, Juliet told reporters that she and Frank were having difficulty resolving the conflict. 'He doesn't want me to work', she said, 'but I do. After working this long and this hard for a career, I'd hate to give it up.' Her manager announced that Juliet would continue working and that he was negotiating a new contract for her with 20th Century-Fox.

Frank was in New York at the time, shooting interior scenes in Madison Square Garden for his independent production of *The Manchurian Candidate*. A columnist asked him about the statements from back in Hollywood that Juliet would continue working after their marriage. 'Irresponsible people are saying those things', Frank replied. 'She's *not* going to do any work. I'd rather not have it.' And, he added, he expected Juliet to 'just walk away from' her contract with Fox.

But Juliet refused, and that was the end of that.

A short time after the engagement was broken, Frank reportedly told friends, "I'll never again be married to a woman who works. I want a wife, a woman who'll have my dinner ready when I arrive home at night. With Ava, half the time she wasn't home from the studio. Even when she was, she had to study her lines for the next day.'

There was another aspect to Frank's inability or disinclination to settle into marriage. In part, it helps explain why his marriages and near-marriages have failed. When Frank Sinatra Jr. was just beginning his own singing career, going out on the road with the old Tommy Dorsey Band, his father sat him down for a long talk. And he told his son that an audience is just like a woman. To romance her and to win her you must give everything inside of you, you must focus all your energies on her until everything else becomes secondary. Unstated was the obvious corollary: Any other woman in his life could only destroy his relationship with his first love, his audiences. And it is this intense love Sinatra gives to his audiences which enabled him to become the greatest entertainer most of us have ever seen and which has helped him endure for thirty-five years.

Frank's relationship with Marilyn picked up again. To close friends, Marilyn would even comment wryly about Sinatra's sexual demands, which both flattered and excited her. One afternoon, a few months before her death in August, 1962, Marilyn was showing her housekeeper photographs taken on Sinatra's yacht shortly after they'd returned from a cruise, and she said, 'I don't think I'll give him copies of the pictures. I think I've already given him enough.'

Frank and Marilyn seemed to be much more than occasional lovers – they were friends in an industry in which there are few real friends. From the moment he grew close to Marilyn, Frank expended a large amount of energy bolstering her very shaky emotional foundations. He was the kind of man who recognized some of the weaknesses in Marilyn which made her appear to so many to be emotionally unbalanced; he went out of his way to force Marilyn to recognize her own weaknesses so that she could attempt to override them. Frank had the remarkable ability to cut through her self-indulgence and flights of self-pitying fantasy and bring her back down to reality. Marilyn frequently illustrated this ability in Sinatra she so deeply appreciated by telling friends about the night she had dinner in Sinatra's home. She was, she said, describing to the other guests her very, very sad childhood, the orphanages and foster homes she went through and suffered in, dramatizing it quite a bit for the effect. Sinatra said quietly, 'Oh, no, not that again.' She later told friends that she'd been devastated by the remark at first, but then, after thinking about it, she realized Frank was probably correct and that he'd done it for her own good.

Frank and Marilyn dated occasionally right up to her death, even during the time she was President John F. Kennedy's lover. And Attorney General Robert Kennedy's lover. A few months before she died (of an overdose of barbiturates that was officially called a probable suicide but that some investigators insist was murder), Marilyn had been fired by her studio for prolonged absences from the set of *Something's Got to Give*. She was depressed about the firing for a time, but when composer Jule Styne told her he was planning to make a film of the novel *A Tree Grows in Brooklyn* with her and Sinatra in the lead roles, she became excited about the project. Especially, she said, because she had always wanted to make a film with Frank. In Hollywood, among those close to Sinatra, it is said with some authority that he was promoting this project because he knew that the best thing for Marilyn, after her disastrous dismissal by her studio, was to get back to work. In the weeks before Marilyn died, Frank was using his very considerable influence with producers, directors, and the executives at Fox to persuade the studio to rehire her. The studio had finally agreed, but Marilyn died before a new contract could be executed.

By the time Sinatra met, romanced, and married the childlike Mia Farrow, at the age of fifty, he had become much larger than life. He was not merely a man and an entertainer, but The Man, The Leader, The King, The Chairman of the Board. He was the senior swinger of the nation, outraging tradition and convention with his antics, his romances, his violent swings in mood from enormous generosity to saloon brawls; he was even considered 'dangerous' to democratic institutions because of his flirtation with John Kennedy and his domination of the Clan and much of Hollywood, Las Vegas, and the entertainment industry. Despite the changing tastes of younger record buyers who were spending millions on rock and roll, his popularity with the mass audiences was greater than it had ever been, greater even than in those early days of swooning bobby-soxers. He had, by now, constructed the financial base to guarantee the independence and influence he seems to have sought ever since being dropped by his agency, his film studio, and his record company in those dark days before *Eternity*.

The base was called Sinatra Enterprises, housed in a sumptuous bungalow on the Warner Brothers lot where the most prominent decorative effects in his office were a bust of Frank sculptured by Jo Davidson in 1944 and inscribed photographs of the previous four Democratic presidents. Sinatra Enterprises consisted of Reprise Records, a firm in which Frank had a one-third interest and Warner Brothers two-thirds; Artanis Productions, one of Sinatra's several motion picture production companies; Cal Jet Airway, a small charter outfit; and a real estate firm with extensive holdings in California and Nevada, including 50 percent ownership in the Cal-Neva Lodge at Lake Tahoe and a 9 percent interest in the Sands in Las Vegas. (Sinatra's licence to operate the gambling casinos at both resorts was surrendered in 1963 after charges were brought against him because of his Mafia associations, but Frank was permitted to retain, and lease the hotel facilities at Cal-Neva.) Frank's worth at this time, late in 1964, was estimated at about $20 million, his annual gross between three and four million.

Although his fortune was rather modest compared to those of Texas oil millionaires, 'Frank lives like royalty', said a friend, producer William Goetz. Like Hollywood royalty, in any case. Sinatra had four homes: a rented ten-room house in Beverly Hills; a rented five-room apartment on Manhattan's East Side; a penthouse overlooking Grosvenor Square in London; and his near-mansion in Palm Springs, a three-bedroom main house with a pair of round five-room guest houses sheltered behind growths of oleander.

Sinatra was rarely alone during this period. As in the days immediately after the breakup of his marriage to Ava and his sudden spurt back to superstar status, he seemed unable to face up to himself, to be alone with his interior demons. Around him, besides one woman 'companion' or another, were always his sizable retinue of friends, employees, hangers-on, and hangers on the hangers-on. They've been characterized variously as the Clan, the Rat Pack, childish fools and hoodlums, but to a man and woman they characterized themselves as being very special people – those who know Sinatra, travel with him, drink with him, fight alongside him. And are always loyal to him and responsive to his needs and whims. As one of them said of him, 'If he were Jewish, he'd be Moses.'

It was into this semi-religious, semi-juvenile pack that Mia

Farrow was suddenly propelled when Sinatra took an interest in her. They met in October, 1964, on the 20th Century-Fox lot where she was working on the TV serial, *Peyton Place,* and he was working in *Von Ryan's Express.* One day she wandered over to Sinatra's set to visit a friend, John Leyton, a young English actor. 'I had some time off', Mia later told a writer, 'and I was fooling around the *Von Ryan* set, climbing up in the rafters. I remember that Edward Mulhare was there, and Frank was climbing out of one of the freight cars. I was embarrassed and wanted to get out of their way.'

She was nineteen then; Sinatra's riot-provoking appearance at the New York Paramount had come precisely twenty years earlier, months before Mia was even born. But now Mia was a striking young woman. Although she was solemn and round-shouldered, and so slight she seemed no more than a child, her voice was whispery soft, the bony structure of her face was fascinating, and her splash of long golden hair was absolutely stunning.

'Who is that girl?' Sinatra asked Leyton.

John called Mia over and introduced them. Like any other Hollywood woman, Mia was set a-tremble (her word) at meeting Frank Sinatra. 'I couldn't believe it when he asked me to come down to the commissary for a cup of coffee', she later told friends.

And John Leyton remembers that Mia was so nervous that when she went to place her purse on the table, she missed it by a foot and it tumbled to the floor. Sinatra leaped to his feet, scooped everything back into the bag, and placed it on the table. 'He asked me to a screening of one of his pictures and of course I went', Mia later said. 'I liked him instantly. He rings true. He is what he is.'

The first public awareness of a possible new romantic interest in Sinatra's life came at the end of November, when columnist Sheilah Graham disclosed that he'd been calling Mia on the *Peyton Place* set. Sinatra's office dismissed the rumours by saying he was simply discussing making a film with Mia. But those 'discussions' became week-ends at Sinatra's desert home, quiet affairs, with none of Frank's usual loud and boisterous friends to mar the intimacy.

They made their first public appearance together at a Hollywood charity luncheon in the spring of 1965. The columnists printed 'inside' stories that they would soon be married, that Sinatra had really fallen in love with her, and that Mia, as was to be expected, had gone wild over him. When asked about the possible marriage, Maureen O'Sullivan, Mia's mother, replied, 'Marry Mia? It would make better sense if he married me.' Dean Martin was forced to phone Frank to deny he had sent a telegram bearing his name which said, 'I have a case of Scotch in the house that's older than Mia Farrow.' And comedian Jack E. Leonard had high praise for Sinatra's choice of his next wife because she didn't drink or smoke – 'She's still teething.'

Frank ignored the public ridicule about his being involved with a woman thirty years his junior, a woman younger than two of his children. He continued to pursue her. Friends say he asked her to marry him some time in the spring of 1965, but she said she was too young and didn't particularly care for the quality of his friends. She told one of her friends around this time, 'Frank's nasty little chums bore me. All they know how to do is tell dirty stories, break furniture, pinch waitresses' asses, and bet on the horses.'

It was significant that, coincidental or not, Sinatra began seeing far less of his brassy ring-a-ding-dinging buddies from the Clan and began inviting more debonair and sophisticated people to his parties. Replacing the Clan were Rosalind Russell and her husband, Freddie Brisson, Claudette Colbert and her husband, Dr Joel Pressman, producer Bill Goetz and his wife, and others of the more conservative side of Hollywood and Palm Springs. Mia's mother said, 'Many of Mia's present friends are the same ones she has known much of her life. The people she sees now with Frank were guests in our home when she was a little girl.' Sinatra appeared to be bending to Mia's needs more than he had ever before done with any woman.

But still she would not marry him. Through all of 1965, his friends say, he tried to persuade her to become his third wife, but she resisted. Their relationship was more than a year old when Frank celebrated his fiftieth birthday on 12th December 1965. Some gossip columnists made a big thing over the fact that Frank's first wife, Nancy, gave him a party at the Beverly Hills Hotel and did not invite Mia. That night, the gossips maintained, Mia was so angry and upset that she hacked off her long hair in a temper tantrum. Actually, Mia told friends she understood why she couldn't attend Frank's party: Not only would it have been coarse of Frank to bring his girlfriend to what was basically a family affair, but most of all it would have meant weeks of headlines approaching the hysteria of the Ava Gardner days. When his official birthday party ended, Frank met Mia for a private celebration and gave *her* a couple of presents – a white horse and a diamond bracelet. (And when he had seen her new hairdo, a couple of days before his birthday, Frank said he liked it very much; apparently he did, according to some of his friends.)

Then, for three months the following spring, Mia and Frank stopped seeing each other. The reasons are still not clear to friends. Some say he was angry that she had cut her hair and now looked like a young boy, but that doesn't seem to be anywhere near the truth. Other friends say Frank's children and his first wife were upset that he was seriously involved with such a young woman. Still others insist Mia grew weary of all the attention Frank paid to his children – recalling the remarks of Jill St John, one of Frank's steadies for a time, that 'Frank will never get married because Nancy Senior and the kids are still Numero Uno with him.' Whatever the cause, the romance appeared to be over. Sinatra resumed his Clan-life and told friends his infatuation was ended. If she calls, he told his pals in Jilly's, his favourite New York hangout, I'm not in, I don't want to talk to her.

Mia began dating other men – Eddie Fisher, Michael Caine, and her old friend, writer Leonard Gersh. Frank didn't seem to mind this kind of competition, apparently dismissing these men as safe little playmates for Mia. But then director Mike Nichols began dating her. A literate, witty, and urbane man, Nichols most definitely did not fit Sinatra's concept of a safe companion for his woman. When

Mia turned up in Rome with Nichols, Frank reportedly grew worried, or jealous.

She never did call him to patch things up, as friends say Frank expected. She won the test of wills. Frank called her at her mother's apartment in New York when she returned from Rome. According to friends who were present when he made the call from Jilly's bar, Frank said, 'I haven't heard from you. Are you ill?' The friends couldn't hear her response. But in a moment Sinatra said, 'I'm taking a few friends to see *The Odd Couple* tomorrow night. I may buy it for a film. Want to come along?' Mia agreed and Frank, who didn't have one ticket to the Broadway smash, made a few fast calls to buy a batch for his spur-of-the-moment theatre party.

They were married on 19th July 1966, in Las Vegas. Only four weeks after the wedding Mia suffered her first publicly reported upset when Frank, from the stage of the Sands, made his crack about marrying 'a broad I can cheat on'. Yet for the first half-year the marriage seemed to work rather well; friends said Mia actually changed Sinatra in a lot of ways. Brad Dexter, the actor who helped save Frank from drowning and became his bodyguard and an executive in his companies, told a writer, 'I've seen a softening in Frank's attitude, a gentleness that he rarely displayed before ... And he doesn't have to call people in the middle of the night, like before, to come and keep him company, to go out drinking with him. Frank was always a lonely guy, but I've seen a change come over him since he met Mia. He doesn't seem to have the old problems. He certainly doesn't drink as much as he used to.'

For a time, it seemed as if Frank were indulging Mia. For example, he would often take her to the Daisy Club, a private Los Angeles discothèque for the younger Hollywood set, rock music blaring over the speakers and kids dancing to rhythms that Sinatra the balladeer abhors. Yet Frank would sit quietly at a ringside table with a friend or two, nursing a drink, while Mia danced exuberantly with some of her friends, writer Leonard Gersh, actors Jack Haley Jr or Roddy McDowell. And Frank always seemed out of place.

Young Haley told a writer, 'When the mood comes on her, Frank allows Mia to visit the Daisy. He's very patient. He'll sit there looking bored or talking to friends, but he knows she's having fun dancing and being around people her own age. It's unusual, because Frank couldn't care less about the Daisy and he doesn't do all those rock dances Mia loves so much. Mia can dance with anyone she likes, as long as she knows it's someone Frank approves of. These young people can never really be friends of his, but he knows them. I think he's checked them out pretty carefully.'

A few months after the marriage, Maureen O'Sullivan talked about the problems confronting her daughter. 'Marrying Frank Sinatra, the greatest living entertainer, has put Mia in a rather difficult position', she told a Hollywood writer. 'She's afraid of saying the wrong thing, as I am, and she avoids personal references, even with me. I think that endears her to Frank.'

If Mia was at first overwhelmed by the legend of her husband, the awe didn't seem to last very long, friends say. Mia soon began asserting herself publicly, telling Frank in front of his friends what she thought of some of his antics. At the Sands one night, Frank threw a box of cup cakes at a couple of his buddies, splattering the very expensive gown worn by a woman at an adjoining table. Mia rebuked him. 'Oh Frank, you're being so childish', she said.

Sinatra seemed hurt for a moment. Then, as if to show his friends he wasn't taking any of *that* sort of lip from his woman, he scooped a handful of ice cubes from a bowl in the centre of the table and hurled them among his guests. Mia was not cowed by his reaction. She again scolded him. 'That's not only childish, it's dangerous. You could knock someone's eyes out.' Sinatra got up and stalked out.

One of Mia's friends told me, 'I think it all began to fall apart when Mia was in London and Berlin the spring after they were married. She was filming *A Dandy in Aspic* with Laurence Harvey. The press agents for the film did what press agents have always done – they sent out pictures of Mia and Harvey in a restaurant and in a couple of clubs. When Frank saw them in the papers he went wild. He phoned Mia – he was working at the Fontainebleau in Miami – and just bawled the hell out of her.'

Mia caught the next plane to Florida and stayed with Frank for forty-eight hours to try and show him that she loved him and would risk breaking her film contract to prove it. Frank practically ignored her.

'He gave me only a half-hour of his time', Mia later complained. 'And that was with his friends around. I never had a moment alone with him. All he did was lecture me for a while. You know, "When people see pictures like those they jump to conclusions. I don't want anyone jumping to any conclusions." I tried to tell him it was just publicity crap, but he wouldn't listen.'

The final break came as a result of another film in which Mia was working, *Rosemary's Baby*. William Castle, the film's producer, has said, 'While Mia was filming *Baby* Frank gave her an ultimatum. Unless she walked off the picture, he would divorce her. Mia made the choice. She finished the film, because it was the finest role of her life.'

Castle says that Sinatra was in New York filming *The Detective,* in which Mia had a role. He wanted her to leave Hollywood where she was filming and fly to New York. 'If Mia had done that', Castle says, 'we would have had to shut down the production. Sinatra called me personally from New York. He was very pleasant about it but asked when Mia would be finished with *Rosemary's Baby*. I told him the truth, that we were behind in our schedule. Sinatra said, "Well, I'm going to call off your picture." I said, "Frank, that's silly." And Frank replied, "No, that's the way I feel. I've waited long enough." '

On the morning of Tuesday, 21st November, Mia told her co-star in *Baby*, John Cassavetes, that she was planning a Thanksgiving Day dinner for Frank, two days later. She laughed. 'I almost burned the house down learning to cook', she said, 'but now I'm good enough to make a whole Thanksgiving dinner.'

That afternoon Frank left their home in Beverly Hills and flew off in his private jet to his desert place in Palm Springs. The next day his lawyer, Mickey Rudin, called Mia and told

her that Frank was about to release a public announcement:
His marriage to Mia was ended after 16 months. Mia thought
it was a joke until she reached Frank's press agent, who
read her the statement.

Some years later Nancy Sinatra Junior gave a magazine
writer her version of the day her father's marriage ended.
Nancy recalled, 'The day that Daddy and Mia separated I
was shooting a commercial. I'd had a terrible dream the night
before. I dreamt that Mia had been shot. The next morning
I tried to get Daddy. I called him at home. But I couldn't
get him all day until about 5:30. He told me what had
happened. They had separated. They were just *crushed,*
the two of them.'

Nancy, who is four years older than Mia, apparently had
some understanding of what her father's wife had been required to put up with. A few months before the Sinatras
separated, Nancy commented on television about her father's
boisterous and often crude circle of locker-room-type buddies.
'Sometimes, when he is with his friends', she said, 'they carry
on like a bunch of kids. And it's great, they're having a
marvellous time. But that bothers me a little.'

For that criticism, mild though it was, Nancy incurred her
father's displeasure. Sinatra has always refused to recognize
gradations in loyalty – it is absolute or irrelevant. His
daughter's lapse was a blow to him. He reportedly stopped
talking to her for three days. For Nancy, the favourite of
his three children, that was punishment enough.

After the breakup of his third marriage, Sinatra again
began to escort some of the younger and more available
Hollywood women, many of them from among his leading
ladies. He was seen with Lee Remick, Jill St John, Deborah
Kerr, and dozens of others. And then, finally, he seemed to
have settled down somewhat with Barbara Marx. At this
writing there are rumours that they will eventually marry
or, in fact, have already been secretly married. The basic
theme of the rumours, especially when promoted by Barbara's
friends, is: Now that Frank is sixty all the young girls who

still chase him and try to climb into his bed are getting to be boring; he's taking great delight in being a grandfather; he's working hard as an entertainer and businessman, and when the day has ended and his buddies go home, he needs a woman he can talk to, a woman he can share his fabulous life with, because even if a man has $50 million it isn't much good if there's no woman to share it with. And that woman is Barbara Marx.

Even Sinatra's ageing uncle, Lawrence Garaventi, joins the chorus, hinting and stating flatly that Frank and Barbara will marry or have already been married. Garaventi recently said, 'Barbara has changed Frank completely. He doesn't play around any more, he doesn't fool around with other women. Never . . . Frank has suddenly sort of grown up a lot . . . he's matured.'

Greg Tyler, who has floated around in Hollywood and international celebrity circles for a decade and claims he was punched by Sinatra in Monte Carlo on 6th August 1972, asserts that he has been told by the most reliable sources in that set that Frank and Barbara were married on the day of that altercation. It took place in their suite at the Hotel de Paris, Tyler asserts. Actor Vince Edwards and Jilly Rizzo were their witnesses. And before flying off to a honeymoon on Capri, Sinatra punched Tyler on the dance floor of the hotel in retaliation for an insult, Tyler says. He's written about it in his memoirs, *Everyone Is a Star*.

Frank Sinatra, on women: 'If I had had as many affairs as some people claim, right now I would be speaking from a jar in the Harvard Medical School . . . I'm supposed to have a Ph.D. on the subject of women, but the truth is I've flunked more often than not. I'm very fond of women. I like women. But like all men, I don't understand them. . . .

'A bartender once told me a nice story. He was closing his joint down and some guys were looking into their sauce and I guess they were playing one of my tunes on the juke-box. It must have been something like "One For My Baby". Anyway, at the end of the song some drunk looks up from his glass and says, "I wonder who *he* listens to?"

'I feel I'm a fairly good provider. All I ask from a wife is that she look after me. And I'll see that she is looked after. I don't feel that I've been a demanding man, but in some respects I'm a hard man to live with. I live my life certain ways that I could never change for a woman. . . .

'Women? They're beautiful. But just a little hard to make out.'

CHAPTER 4

Ever since the rumours that Mafia man Willie Moretti helped Frank Sinatra get out of the extortionate contract held by Tommy Dorsey, Frank has been making periodic headlines because of his friendships with the elite of the American Mafia. Although those headlines have never affected his popularity, they have hurt him financially and, what is worse for a man with his need to achieve national influence or the illusion of such influence, have caused presidents and presidential candidates to publicly disassociate themselves from him.

As has already been pointed out, Sinatra has always maintained that his contacts with hoodlums is something he cannot avoid because as a famous personality he brushes elbows with all sorts of people, including 'presidents and kings'. In effect, Sinatra claims his only contact with the Mafia has been in saloons where they force themselves upon him because, like so many men and women, they want to know the most famous entertainer in the world.

'Sure I know those guys', Sinatra once conceded to a writer who asked him about his friends in the national crime syndicate. 'You can't be in the nightclub business for more than twenty-five years without taking a drink with a few of the boys now and then. But I'm not *involved* with them, if that's what you mean.'

It is true there has never been the slightest evidence that Sinatra has ever been involved in business dealings with the mob, that he has ever done anything illegal, that he has benefitted in any way from his mob associates. But there is substantial documentation which shows that Sinatra has for three decades or more numbered among his friends some of the most notorious *Mafiosi* in the nation. And not simply as drinking companions on rare occasions.

Perhaps, as some friends have always said through the years, these goons provide a certain glamour for the adolescent which still appears to lurk within Sinatra. Perhaps Frank may indeed have always nurtured a secret desire to be a hood, as Bing Crosby once said, and is fulfilling that desire in the only manner available to him – vicariously, through repeated contacts with hoodlums. Perhaps Frank's psychiatrist could come up with a more Freudian explanation.

Whatever the reason, Sinatra has been associating with Mafia men at least since the earliest days of his stardom, according to the files of a dozen investigative agencies from Washington, D.C., to California. For example, in the Justice Department files is a copy of a telegram sent to Sinatra in 1950 by Willie Moretti. The story of Willie's activity in getting Frank out of a contract may have been nothing more than a rumour. But Moretti obviously believed he could lecture Frank, as a father might, about marital responsibility. Willie's cable, sent when Sinatra was chasing Ava across two continents and was trying to persuade Nancy to give him a divorce, read: 'I am very much surprised what I have been reading in the newspapers between you and your darling wife. Remember you have a decent wife and children. You should be very happy. Regards to all. Willie Moore.' (Moore was Willie's *nom-de-gang*.)

But Moretti was a minor Mafia figure compared to some of the other men with whom Sinatra has been associated. Lucky Luciano, for one. A couple of days before Charlie Lucky died of a heart attack in Naples in 1962, Italian police searched his apartment hoping to get evidence that he was the leader of a massive international heroin-smuggling business. About the only item of interest they found was a gold cigarette case with the inscription: TO CHARLIE, FROM HIS PAL FRANK SINATRA.

It was the word *pal* which first created headlines about Sinatra's contacts with *Mafiosi*. Lucky Luciano was the brilliant Mafia strategist who succeeded in assassinating the leaders of two opposing factions of the American Mafia in the early thirties. He then put together a criminal cartel of Italian, Jewish, Irish, and other ethnic gangster groups which became the American crime syndicate and which continues to function as an international criminal organization to this day. Luciano was the undisputed leader of the cartel. Because it was impossible to convict him of any substantive crime, he was framed on a compulsory prostitution charge by New York special prosecutor Thomas E. Dewey, who would go on to become governor of New York and almost win the presidential election in 1948. Convicted in 1936, Charlie spent almost ten years in prison. His sentence had been for a minimum of thirty years. But with the assistance of several easily bought officials in U.S. Navy Intelligence and in the New York prosecutor's office, it was made to appear that, from his prison cell, Luciano almost single-handedly conquered Sicily for the Allies in World War II. And the honourable Mr Dewey, governor of the state at the end of the war, was either bought or blackmailed by Luciano's Mafia partners. Dewey paroled Luciano, with the proviso that he accept deportation.

Luciano agreed to the conditions of parole after extracting from Dewey and from other political figures a secret understanding that he would be permitted to return quietly to the United States in a few years. He was sent to Italy in 1946. Early in 1947, to prepare for his return to the United States, Charlie flew to Cuba. As soon as he settled into a suite in the Hotel Nacional (whose casino he owned in partnership with Meyer Lansky, Frank Costello, and other crime syndicate leaders), Charlie summoned the élite of the American Mafia to fly down to see him and discuss expediting his return to America. He booked thirty-six hotel suites to hold them all.

One of the few non-Mafia personalities to fly to Havana and visit Lucky was the idol of the American bobby-soxers, Frank Sinatra. A report of the Federal Narcotics Bureau states that Sinatra flew from Miami to Havana with Rocco and Joseph Fischetti of Chicago, cousins of Al Capone and high-ranking members of Capone's old mob.

When the story of Sinatra's visit was later revealed, some newspaper columnists claimed that the singer was carrying a briefcase with 'two million dollars in small bills' as a favour for the Fischettis, who didn't want to be embarrassed should they be searched and the money found. Sinatra denied the charge and quite correctly pointed out that two million in small bills would weigh a couple of tons. Some sleuths in the Narcotics Bureau, which had fed the story to the newspapers, probably weighed all the small bills they could round up because the Bureau soon announced it had made a mistake; the bills were very large ones and the Fischettis carried the bags themselves. Despite that official error, there is no doubt most of the mobsters travelling to pay their respects to Luciano did bring him large sums of money. Charlie later talked about it to friends and said the money had been his return on investments in various legal and illegal enterprises in America.

A funny thing happened to some young Sinatra fans while he was in Havana, according to another Narcotics Bureau report. His arrival had been noted in the Havana press, and fans flocked to the Nacional for his autograph or just a glimpse of their idol. Among them was a full Catholic school class of young and proper girls, with a nun as a chaperone. The hotel staff treated the nun with great deference, and she and her charges were delivered up to Lucky's penthouse apartment, where Sinatra was believed to be visiting. To everyone's ill fortune, Luciano had thrown a rather wild party the night before, the official report continues. When the nun and her girls reached the suite the door stood ajar. She timidly ventured into the place with her girls. And they were all duly shocked by the chaos they saw. Bottles littered the floor, lingerie was draped over furniture and lamps. A number of men and women, most of them rather nude, lay where they had collapsed. The nun and the girls beat a fast retreat.

The incident was reported to the mother superior, who wrote a pained letter to her bishop. This gentleman was quite angry and he was preparing a pastoral letter on the evils of such men as Luciano, for delivery to all Cuban churches and copies to the press, when the Narcotics Bureau agents learned about it. The Bureau didn't want a scandal over Luciano's presence in Havana, for it was interested in collecting information on his meeting with American mobsters. Narcotics agents persuaded the bishop to delay his pastoral letter, promising that when enough information had been collected, the Cuban government would be forced to deport Luciano.

But then newspaper columnist Robert Ruark happened to fly to Havana for a vacation. One day, quite by accident, he saw Luciano in a restaurant with a New York society woman who had recently divorced her husband. Ruark promptly began to write a series of articles about Luciano's presence in Havana, pointing out that the increased use of narcotics in American cities was probably connected in some way with Luciano's residence so near to the United States.

The Narcotics Bureau began feeding Ruark and other reporters who flocked to Havana details about Luciano's visitors, including Sinatra. The head of the Bureau, Henry Anslinger (Ass-slinger, Luciano called him with much hatred), ordered the release of the information on Sinatra for two reasons. Anslinger abhorred Sinatra's liberal politics and was upset that the singer had been given a special Academy Award for his 1945 anti-bigotry short film, *The House I Live In*. And Anslinger found in the combination of Sinatra and Luciano a perfect way to generate enormous headlines for his agency, then about to go before Congress on its annual trek for increased appropriations. Ruark and other writers for the right-wing press, despising Sinatra's politics as much as Anslinger did, printed everything the Bureau could supply them about Frank and invented a few details of their own.

But the fact remained that Sinatra had indeed accompanied two high-ranking men of the Mafia to Havana and had visited Lucky Luciano. The publicity generated by that visit caused Sinatra to offer an explanation. 'I was brought up to shake a man's hand when I am introduced to him without first investigating his past', Frank said. When writers shouted that *everyone* in America knew about Luciano's past, Sinatra offered a further explanation. He said he had bumped into one of the Fischetti brothers in Miami and casually mentioned that he was planning to spend a few days in Havana. The Fischetti brothers were also going to Havana and they changed their reservations so they could be on the same plane with Sinatra.

When he got to Havana, Frank said, he was introduced to a large group of people. They invited him to join them at dinner. Only after joining them did he realize Lucky Luciano was also a guest. 'It suddenly struck me that I was laying myself open to criticism by remaining at the table, but I could think of no way to leave in the middle of dinner without creating a scene', Sinatra said.

The Narcotics Bureau reports, however, state that Sinatra did not simply have dinner with Luciano on one occasion, but spent four days with the *Mafioso* and his gangster friends, gambling with them and partying with them until the early morning hours. The report did say, quite clearly, that when the mobsters held 'business' meetings, Sinatra was not with them.

Sinatra's friendship with Rocco Fischetti continued through 1964, when the Chicago mobster died. Over the years, Sinatra often visited the Fischetti home during trips to Chicago. Joe Fischetti has been Sinatra's companion whenever the singer appears in Miami Beach. In fact, according to sworn depositions given in Dade County Circuit Court, Florida, in 1968, when Sinatra entertains at the Fontaine-bleau Hotel, Joe Fischetti goes on the payroll at a thousand dollars a month.

The Luciano incident had become only a dim memory by 1960, when Sinatra became an active and very welcome supporter of John F. Kennedy. The singer appeared at benefits to raise money for Kennedy, urged the liberals among the Hollywood set to forget their fears and become involved in politics, and he joined Senator Kennedy on several campaign trips. After the election, it was Sinatra who escorted Jackie Kennedy to the Inaugural Gala, which he staged the evening before the official inauguration. With tickets priced from $100 to $10,000 for the privilege of seeing some of the finest entertainers in America (plus Sir Laurence Olivier) perform at the National Guard Armory, Sinatra's production erased almost one and a half million dollars in Democratic campaign debts in a single night. It was an unforgettable preview night for the Kennedy Camelot years and, except for Republican-orientated newspaper writers who attacked Sinatra for everything from lacking dignity to failing to provide 'proper cultural tone', it seemed plain that Frank was going to bring a large dose of glamour to a White House that under Eisenhower had been mired in the cultural bog of Lawrence Welk and Fred Waring.

The next night, after Kennedy and Vice President Johnson had been sworn into office and while five Inaugural Balls were underway, the new president appeared at a private party given by Frank at the Statler-Hilton. The following morning Frank and Peter Lawford and his wife – Kennedy's sister – breakfasted with Robert Kennedy and then attended his induction as attorney general. That evening they flew with Joe Kennedy, the family patriarch, in his private plane for a brief vacation at Palm Beach.

According to close friends and to FBI reports that have slowly been pried out of the files, Sinatra played a special role in John Kennedy's life. Although he was young and wealthy, 'the most powerful leader in the Western world', Jack Kennedy was star struck. And he was also consistently unfaithful to his wife. Even as a senator, Kennedy frequently slipped away from his duties to romance Washington secretaries, party workers, newspaper-women, and the wife of a well-known diplomat; he also dallied with an occasional actress during trips to Peter Lawford's beach house in California. Now, with the entire world open to him as president, John Kennedy began a year-long affair with Marilyn Monroe.

From all the information available, Marilyn deliberately set out to seduce Kennedy by drawing close once more to Sinatra and by joining his circle, which included Lawford. It was actually Lawford, friends say, who introduced Marilyn and President Kennedy, apparently in New York about five months after the inauguration. They immediately became lovers. Their affair was pursued in New York's Carlyle Hotel, the Beverly Hills Hotel, Lawford's home in Santa Monica, and even in Kennedy's private plane, the *Caroline*.

It was also Sinatra, according to investigators, who introduced Kennedy to a blue-eyed, raven-haired, Hollywood party girl named Judith Campbell. The relationship between Kennedy and Judith was very briefly and murkily commented upon in the Senate Intelligence Committee report on CIA assassination plots because Mrs Campbell, while she was one of the president's several extramarital interests, was also intimate with two major Mafia figures who were part of the CIA's plot to kill Fidel Castro. But the CIA report was so vague it didn't even mention the gender of Kennedy's 'close friend' who was associated with two Mafia men.

The Campbell liaison, according to her story and to independent investigators, began in Las Vegas in February, 1960, when the senator was in the midst of his campaign to win the Democratic party presidential nomination. Kennedy had flown into Vegas on 7th February for a rest from campaigning. By prearrangement he met Sinatra and other members of the Clan – Sammy Davis, Dean Martin, Peter Lawford, and a few others. The lot of them were in town filming *Ocean's 11* by day and breaking up the mainroom crowds at the Sands by night with an impromptu Clan act. After hours, they partied in their suites upstairs. Even before Kennedy joined the crowd, they assumed, most naturally, that he'd like female companionship and it was arranged. Sinatra, it has been widely reported, put in a call to Los Angeles and asked the lissome 26-year-old Judy to fly over immediately. She did, turning up at the Sands at a party attended by Sinatra's crowd, a lot of available women, and Jack Kennedy.

Eventually, she found her way to Senator Kennedy and they later went off to his suite for the night.

Judy, living on a small alimony but mostly by her wits, was also intimate with Sam Giancana, the Chicago Mafia boss, and with Johnny Roselli, his West Coast and Las Vegas counterpart. At the time both of them were working for the CIA, attempting to line up a Cuban Mafia associate to assassinate Fidel Castro. Judy claimed that she met Giancana in Miami Beach a month after becoming intimate with Kennedy, having been introduced to the *Mafioso* by the friend she refuses to name publicly but who Federal sources say was Sinatra. She met Roselli even later than that, she says. Roselli, however, says he met her in 1958 and dated her frequently over the next couple of years.

Whatever the truth, it is certain that Judith maintained a steady relationship with Kennedy even after he became president, while at the same time being intimate with Giancana and Roselli. By her own account, partially verified by FBI reports, she visited Kennedy at the White House more than twenty times, usually for very private lunches. Senate investigators learned that on one occasion, while she was ensconced in the Fontainebleau Hotel in Miami Beach with Giancana and Roselli, she made a quick trip to Palm Springs to be with Kennedy after he called and asked her to join him. She claimed that she received countless telephone calls from him. She also seemed to have dialled his number quite often; White House logs show that during a fifty-four-week period in 1961 and early 1962 she phoned Kennedy seventy times from her home in Los Angeles, from Oak Park, Illinois – where Giancana lived until his murder in 1975 – and from other spots.

None of the evidence indicates that Giancana or Roselli profited from having a girlfriend who was also a girlfriend of the President of the United States. To the contrary, the Federal pressures on Giancana intensified during the Kennedy years as Bobby Kennedy mounted his Justice Department drive against high Mafia figures.

Ironically, it was Bobby's determination to destroy the Mafia which led to the discovery of Judith's double sex life and, also, to Frank Sinatra's 'humiliation' when the President publicly severed ties with him. In the autumn of 1961, Bobby ordered the FBI to step up its laggardly efforts against organized crime. Until then, J. Edgar Hoover had always denied the existence of the Mafia; there was safer publicity for the FBI in pretending bank robbers and kidnappers were the nation's major crime problem. Bobby Kennedy ended all that. His battle plan was to target a list of forty major hoodlums and have the FBI place them under wiretap surveillance. Giancana's phone was one of those tapped and his friends were identified. Among them were his best girl, singer Phyllis McGuire, and Judith Campbell.

The two women were themselves subjected to investigation, including phone taps, and Judith's home phone records disclosed she had made two phone calls to the private number of President Kennedy's secretary in November, 1961. That information made its way to Hoover, who wrote a memo in February, 1962, warning Bobby Kennedy that a girlfriend of Giancana was phoning the White House, and leaving the rest to the attorney general's imagination.

At first, it appears, Bobby didn't interfere with his brother's sexual activities; the only effect of the Hoover memo was that the President's secretary left orders with the White House switchboard that she would no longer accept calls from Judith Campbell. But the president continued to call her and see her.

Hoover had always been more of a politician than a cop. He permitted the matter to simmer for a month until he determined how to use his information to the best self-advantage. On March 22, prepped by an FBI memorandum detailing the calls to the White House by 'a girlfriend of mobsters', Hoover met the President and some of his aides for lunch. He did not mention the Campbell woman while others were present. At the end of the meeting, alone with the President for a few moments, he showed the memo to Kennedy – thereby displaying his loyalty to his chief and also demonstrating his edge over him.

It isn't known whether Judy's other life surprised President Kennedy, but on the surface some corrective action was taken. The White House logs show one more call from her, about two hours after the Hoover lunch, and then complete silence. Sinatra and his Clan are said also to have been barred from further White House contact.

But that was only on the surface, a public relations illusion in the unlikely event some sort of scandal were made of it all. Senate investigators have turned up evidence that Kennedy continued to see Judy at least until mid-1962, and she claims she last spoke to him at the end of that year. And the 'break' with Sinatra did not actually come until the following year.

Apparently, Jack Kennedy did begin to worry about his lady friend's association with hoodlums and to wonder about Sinatra's role in the entire affair. But he didn't seem to worry too much. It wasn't until some time at the end of 1962, when Kennedy was already beginning to look toward his 1964 re-election campaign, that he decided to check up on Sinatra. It happened when Kennedy was warned by several Democratic leaders and by Bobby that Sinatra, because of his contact with Mafia figures, could become a political liability, a weak spot to be attacked by Republicans. The President asked Bobby to assign some of his agents to look into Sinatra's mob connections. Jack Kennedy reportedly said, 'Just find out whether Frank could be embarrassing to us.'

Bobby ordered the deputy chief of the Organized Crime section, Henry Petersen, to conduct a quiet investigation. The inquiry consisted primarily of collating material on Sinatra already collected by Hoover, who maintained dossiers on practically everyone of fame or influence, and of sending out a few FBI men to gather from local law enforcement agencies more current information on Sinatra, especially in Chicago and Las Vegas. Because it was primarily an information-gathering expedition, not aimed at eventual charges against anyone nor at publicly embarrassing Frank, no wiretap or surveillance techniques were employed, no questions were asked of Frank or his friends and associates.

On 3rd August 1962, Bobby Kennedy received a formal report on Sinatra, nineteen single-spaced pages long. It went into considerable detail about Frank's contacts with several gangsters of note, including the Fischetti brothers, and Giancana and Roselli. The report states that Sinatra had been in contact with ten of the most powerful gangsters in the country in the late fifties and early sixties, and it details the dates when some of these mobsters telephoned Frank's home on his unlisted number. It also describes special favours that Sinatra performed for some of his friends.

One of those favours which was sketched in the report

involved an auto dealer named Peter Epsteen, who had tried to persuade Sinatra to record a radio commercial for his Pontiac agency in Skokie, Illinois, but had no success. Epsteen, the report states, asked the help of Rocco and Joe Fischetti, 'after which Sinatra made the commercial as a favour without charge', according to what Epsteen's former wife had told investigators. The report adds that Sinatra did agree to accept two Pontiacs as a gift from the auto dealer.

The FBI also said it was told by an 'informant' that up to April, 1962, 'Joe Fischetti, under the name of Joe Fisher, had received seventy-one cheques from the Fontainebleau Hotel, each in the amount of $540 (Total: $38,340).' Fischetti received the money, the report indicates, in his role as a 'talent scout' whenever Sinatra appeared at the hotel. That information was at least partially confirmed by depositions given in a suit involving the hotel in 1968.

The investigators also implied that Frank may have been involved with Mafia figures in his business dealings in Nevada, although there was absolutely no proof that this was so. All the 'evidence' FBI agents possessed about any Sinatra-gangster financial arrangements was a phone tap in which Giancana boasted to friends that he owned a percentage of Sinatra's Cal-Neva Lodge. The document also states that Sinatra employed as manager at the lodge a New Jersey underworld figure named Paul Emilio D'Amato. D'Amato's actual job was to protect Giancana's interest in the gambling casino, the report states, again without evidence.

The document on Sinatra concluded:

> Sinatra has had a long and wide association with hoodlums and racketeers which seems to be continuing. The nature of Sinatra's work may, on occasion, bring him into contact with underworld figures, but this cannot account for his friendship and/or financial involvement with people such as Joe and Rocco Fischetti, cousins of Al Capone, Paul Emilio D'Amato, John Formosa, and Sam Giancana, all of whom are on our list of racketeers. No other entertainer appears to be mentioned nearly so frequently with racketeers.
>
> Available information indicates not only that Sinatra

is associated with each of the above-named racketeers but that they apparently maintain contact with one another. This indicates a possible community of interest, involving Sinatra and racketeers in Illinois, Indiana, New Jersey, Florida, and Nevada.

The Federal investigators completely ignored Sinatra's personality, which may be a more reasonable and less sinister explanation for what appears to be a gangster 'community of interest' in which Frank is a member. In brief, two facets of Sinatra's complex person may be at play here. First, he appears to cherish a secret desire to be a hoodlum, or may find hoodlums the last fascinating and glamorous group of people available to him. Second, he must forever play the role of beneficent giver, emulating in his generosity his mother, the 'Lady Godiva' of Hoboken politics. Assuming the truth of what was not proved by the Federal investigation, that Frank cut Giancana into part ownership of the Cal-Neva Lodge, that he did bring mobster friends into his investment opportunities (as he cut in actors, songwriters, producers, and other Hollywood friends), the possibility looms large that such open-handed largesse was simply his manner of rewarding friendship and loyalty, even of gangsters. Foolish and indiscreet, perhaps, but not necessarily proof of genuine Mafia involvement.

The long Justice Department summary of the information compiled about Sinatra led, according to the established wisdom, to a complete break in the once-warm relationship between Frank and the President. In truth, although Bobby Kennedy was urging his brother to sever all ties with Sinatra, the relationship between the President and the entertainer simply went underground. On the surface, the relationship was ended. The President made it appear that he was pulling away from Sinatra when he ostentatiously stayed at Bing Crosby's house in Palm Springs after it had originally been announced he would be a guest in Sinatra's home. But that change of plans was designed solely for public consumption, for political reasons. Privately, John Kennedy continued seeing Sinatra at dinner parties and at more intimate little affairs. JFK was, strangely enough, a groupie, and he wasn't about to give up the companionship of the King of Hollywood.

But some months later, Frank's friendship with Sam Giancana gave Bobby Kennedy further ammunition with which to pressure his brother into dropping Frank from the White House circle of intimates. As part of Bobby's campaign against the Mafia, the FBI assigned a dozen or more agents to keep Giancana under round-the-clock surveillance. A team of agents would park outside Giancana's home through the night and follow him when he went out in the morning. Another team would relieve them and keep Giancana closely tailed through the day. A third team would follow him all evening, in effect 'putting him to bed' as they called it, and then remain parked outside his door until the process began all over again the next day. The FBI's main purpose was pure harassment, on Bobby's orders. Even when the mobster was out playing golf with some of his buddies, the foursome directly behind him and his group was composed of FBI men; when dining in a restaurant, the next table was filled with FBI agents. 'I can't even take a shit without one of those bastards comin' in and holding my pecker', Giancana was heard complaining on one wiretap.

The hounding of Sam Giancana worked so well that the mobster was driven to sue in Federal Court for some relief from the torture. Although he won a minor victory, it didn't do much to end the harassment – the court ruled that everything the FBI was doing as part of its official rackets-busting duties was legal, except that even government agents should not be permitted to hamper a man's golf score by tailing so closely; the court ordered the FBI to permit at least one other set of golfers to be playing between Giancana and his shadows. So the FBI continued following Giancana everywhere, annoying the hell out of him. His golf score kept getting worse.

In desperation Giancana sent one of his aides, Chuck English, to talk to a Justice Department official about arranging a personal meeting between the Chicago gang leader and Attorney General Kennedy, to discuss some relief from the FBI surveillance. And Giancana's emissary said, 'If Kennedy wants to talk he should get in touch with Frank Sinatra to set it up.'

Bobby declined the invitation and went rushing to the President to inform him of this further evidence of Sinatra's friendship with racketeers. Bobby once more demanded that his brother make a real and lasting break with Sinatra. The President, his aides said in later years, simply shrugged and continued to see Frank and his crowd in Los Angeles and Palm Springs.

And then, in September, 1963, came the blackest headlines Sinatra had received because of his Mafia friends since his visit to Lucky Luciano sixteen years before. Those headlines might possibly have caused President Kennedy to finally cut all ties with Sinatra, as Bobby had been demanding, but the President was assassinated in Dallas two months later so the fervour of his loyalty to Sinatra was never tested.

Sinatra, however, displayed a very obstinate loyalty to Giancana as he does to all he considers loyal to him, and he was forced to give up his Nevada casino as a result.

Sinatra's battle with the state of Nevada had its beginnings in 1960, when the state's Gaming Control Board, which supervises casino licences, distributed a 'black book' among casino operators. The volume had eleven sheets of letter-sized paper inside. Each sheet carried the photograph and aliases of one man, plus an FBI file number and at least one local arrest number from some American city. The men named in the book included Sam Giancana, Murray (The Camel) Humphreys, and Marshal Caifano, all of Chicago; Trigger Mike Coppola of New York and Miami; and Joe Sica and Tom Dragna of Los Angeles. The casino operators were told that these men were not to be permitted on the premises of a casino because they were gangsters and they gave Nevada gambling a bad name, and if any licensee did not police his own establishment and keep these men out, he risked the loss of his gambling permit. (It was curious that while the eleven men listed in the slim volume were indeed major crime syndicate figures and that some of them probably had a hidden interest in some casinos, the biggest mobsters and secret owners of Nevada gambling joints, men such as Frank Costello, Meyer Lansky, and Carlo Gambino, were not listed.)

From the time the black book was issued until September, 1963, only one man listed in the book was ever barred from casinos. He was Marshal Caifano, one of Giancana's partners in the Chicago crime syndicate. Caifano apparently decided to test the legality of the order barring him from the casinos. One night early in 1961 he began to circulate openly from one casino to another. Soon, agents of the Gaming Control Board became aware of his presence; they would have had to be blind to miss him. Those agents passed the word to casino operators to bar Caifano, to eject him, to obey the board's orders. The casinos refused. The board then moved all its available agents to the Vegas Strip and began disrupting the operations of casinos in which Caifano had been gambling. They stopped games to check dice and cards, examined roulette wheels, and in general harassed the casino operators. The high-rolling gamblers, nervous with so many police around, began deserting the joints. Caifano, meanwhile, continued his tour. When he arrived at the Desert Inn, he was finally barred. The Gaming Control Board had made its point; the black book was to be treated as Holy Writ.

Everything went back to normal over the next couple of years. Several of the hoodlums on the blacklist appeared at various casinos with no trouble from the owners or from agents of the Gaming Board who were always lurking around. Giancana, in fact, practically commuted between Chicago and Las Vegas, visiting several of the gambling casinos dozens of times. On New Year's Eve, 1960, Vegas historians report, Giancana arrived in town with his girlfriend, Phyllis McGuire, and a party of Chicago mobsters. He established himself and his group in the casino of one of the hotels. An owner of the hotel had a minor argument with Giancana. The gangster ordered the man to 'shut up and get out'. The man, whose name appears on the licence as part-owner of the place, did as he was told. The board took no action on this or any other occasion that a blacklisted mobster visited a casino.

Despite this long record of nonenforcement, Nevada

authorities came down hard on Sinatra because he refused to kick Giancana off the premises of his Cal-Neva Lodge and because, most of all, he insisted that although he might in future obey the board's rule about mobsters, he would not promise that he'd avoid all contact with Giancana *outside* the state of Nevada.

The Sinatra affair began in July, 1963, when Giancana, still smarting under the FBI surveillance, flew out of Chicago for more pleasant climes. Accompanied by Phyllis McGuire, he went to Mexico for a brief vacation. Then, on 17th July Giancana moved into Chalet No. 50 at Cal-Neva, which was Phyllis's residence while she was singing at the hotel.

When Gaming Board agents learned Giancana was living at the lodge, they told the manager that the mobster would have to go. The manager took no action. The chairman of the board, a former newspaper reporter named Edward A. Olsen, called Sinatra to his office for an explanation. Olsen later said Sinatra admitted having seen Giancana at the lodge but denied having invited him there. He promised not to associate with the gang leader in Nevada again, but added that Giancana was a friend and that it was his own business if he wanted to see his friend outside the state.

Olsen replied that it would reflect badly on gambling in the state if Sinatra associated with gangsters while holding a casino licence. Therefore, Sinatra must promise never again to see Giancana, anywhere. Frank refused to make such a promise, and when the meeting ended inconclusively, Olsen ordered his agents to begin amassing evidence for a complaint against Sinatra.

A few days after the meeting, Olsen says, Frank called him at his office and invited him to Cal-Neva for dinner so that they could discuss 'this thing'. Olsen replied that he couldn't accept such an invitation since the board was investigating the lodge. 'But he kept insisting', Olsen later told reporters, 'and I kept refusing. The more I refused the madder he got, until he seemed almost hysterical. He used the foulest language I ever heard in my life.' Finally, according to Olsen's version, Sinatra said that if his invitation was refused he would never talk to anyone from the board again.

Olsen threatened to subpoena Sinatra. And, Olsen said, Frank replied, 'You subpoena me and you're going to get a big fat fuckin' surprise.'

The board soon issued a formal complaint against Sinatra. In it, Olsen charged that Frank used 'obscene and indecent language which was menacing in the extreme and constituted a threat' against Olsen. The official charges also said that 'Frank Sinatra maligned and vilified ... by the use of foul and repulsive language which was venomous in the extreme.'

Frank no doubt exploded because he believed – possibly correctly – that he was being singled out by the board, which had ignored other blacklisted mobsters in the casinos in the past. And when Sinatra blows up, he makes a lasting impression on the object of his anger.

It all came into the open on 11th September 1963, when Olsen issued his formal complaint charging Sinatra with violation of Control Board rules. The complaint read in part:

> The name of said individual, Sam Giancana, under that or other names, was well and unfavourably known to the public press as well as to enforcement agencies so that reports of his activities had appeared in public print for a long time prior to and including July of 1963, and he had been subject of newspaper, magazine, radio, and television reports throughout the United States. Such reports have designated him as one of the twelve overlords in the organization known as 'Cosa Nostra', sometimes known as 'Mafia', which was and is an organization or society dedicated to supervision and control of criminal activities in the United States of America.

The complaint went on to say that Attorney General Kennedy had called the identification of Giancana as a top Mafia boss 'the biggest intelligence breakthrough yet in combating organized crime and racketeering in the United States'. It charged that Giancana was 'known to have been entertained, harboured, and permitted to remain at Cal-Neva Lodge and to receive services and courtesies from the licensee, its representatives, employees, agents, and directors'. Olsen argued that having Giancana as a guest was 'inimical to the public health, safety, morals, good order, and general welfare of the state. . . .'

Olsen further charged that Sinatra 'associated with and spoke to said Sam Giancana . . . and did not request Sam Giancana to leave and made no effort to persuade him to depart . . . Frank Sinatra, principal stockholder, has for a number of years maintained and continued social association with Sam Giancana well knowing his unsavoury and notorious reputation, and has openly stated that he intends to continue such association in defiance' of board regulations.

By law, Sinatra was required to answer the complaint and demonstrate at a public hearing why he should not have his gaming licences revoked. Frank immediately issued statements promising to fight the attempt to revoke his licences in Cal-Neva and the Sands. All of the other casino operators in Nevada lined up behind him, for the men on the blacklist were big gamblers and they always attracted to Vegas only slightly smaller gamblers; they were good for business. But one casino owner reflected the feeling of most observers when he told a magazine writer, 'Had Sinatra behaved like a decent, rational human being, he might have gotten off with a slap on the wrist. But he had to scream at Ed Olsen. Now he's gonna get it.'

A few days before the deadline by which Sinatra had to answer the charges against him, his attorneys went into the board's offices and questioned its members to precisely what evidence they had to prove their charges against Frank. They apparently had a great deal of evidence, because on the night before he was to appear at a board meeting Sinatra issued this statement :

> About six months ago, I decided that my investments and interests were too diversified and that it would be in my best interests to devote most, if not all, of my time to the entertainment industry, not only as an entertainer but as an investor and executive. To achieve this, I instructed my attorney to adopt an

orderly plan to liquidate my non-entertainment industry investments, and merge my interests in the
entertainment industry with one major company so
that I can centralize my activities and investments . . .

As part of that plan I intended to divest myself
completely from any involvement with the gaming industry in Nevada.

I was surprised, hurt, and angered when the Nevada
Gaming Board asked the Nevada Gaming Commission
to revoke my licences to participate in the gaming
industry in Nevada. My immediate reaction was to
contest such recommendation, although it was consistent with my future plans.

However, the Nevada Gaming Control Act specifically provides that a gaming licence is a 'revocable
privilege' which the Nevada gaming officials may grant
or revoke at their discretion and that I had no vested
rights to retain this privilege. . . .

Since I have decided that I belong in the entertainment industry and not in the gaming industry, no
useful purpose would be served by devoting my time
and energies convincing the Nevada gaming officials
that I should be a part of their gaming industry. I
have recently become associated with a major company
in the entertainment industry (Warner Brothers) and in
forming that association I have agreed to devote my
full time and efforts to that company's activities in the
entertainment industry.

Accordingly, I have instructed my attorney to notify
the Nevada gaming officials that I am withdrawing
from the gaming industry in Nevada. . . .

Sinatra sold his holdings in the Sands and Cal-Neva casinos
for a reported $3.5 million, but was permitted to continue
his majority ownership of the Cal-Neva hotel.

Surprisingly, it was Robert Ruark, the columnist who
had most strongly attacked Sinatra for his 1947 trip to
Havana, who now came to his defence. The columnist went
to the heart of the matter when he wrote: 'Any state that
lives off big gambling and its by-products – and I should
not like to mention a high order of harlotry – and which has

paid court to the likes of Bugsy Siegel and Mickey Cohen, is living in the glassiest of parlour houses.'

The bad press Sinatra received over the Nevada incident was quickly transformed into sympathetic headlines in December, 1963, when Frank was thrust into another really deep personal crisis – the kidnapping of his son. Frank Sinatra, Jr., nineteen years old and singing on his own for seven months with the regrouped Tommy Dorsey Band, was kidnapped from Harrah's Club, near the Cal-Neva, and held for three days while his abductors conducted ransom negotiations with his father. At first the gossips said it was all a publicity stunt to promote the young singer the way Daddy had promoted many of his girlfriends. But it was the real thing, and it terrified the elder Sinatra. 'I used to worry constantly about some nuts kidnapping my kids', he said later, 'but I haven't thought about it for years because the kids are all grown up.' Sinatra paid $240,000 ransom, his son was released, and the kidnappers were quickly caught and most of the money returned. The three inexpert criminals received long prison sentences.

Sinatra stayed out of national politics after John Kennedy was murdered in Dallas. He apparently blamed Bobby Kennedy for at least some of his troubles in Nevada. It didn't take much imagination to understand that a good part of the evidence amassed against Sinatra by Nevada officials came from the Justice Department report, a copy of which Bobby gave to the Gaming Control Board. When Kennedy announced that he would seek the Democratic Party nomination for president in 1968, running against Vice President Humphrey, Sinatra came out in support of Humphrey. It was suggested by one interviewer that he was getting revenge for Bobby's opposition to him during the Kennedy presidency, but Sinatra denied it. He was against Bobby for a more important reason, Frank said, 'Because Bobby's not qualified to be president.'

As in John Kennedy's 1960 campaign, Frank's role in the Humphrey drive for the nomination was to raise funds and to lend the candidate some of the glamour he and his Clan possessed. But Frank reportedly had a few problems selling Humphrey to some of his Hollywood friends, who criticized both Sinatra and the Vice President for their support of the war in Vietnam. Sinatra asked Humphrey how he was supposed to justify the position. Humphrey said, 'Refer all inquiries to me.' Sinatra then sent his friends letters telling them to question Humphrey personally about Vietnam. Privately, Frank said he was against the war, but the only prominent dove around was Bobby Kennedy and he damned well wasn't going to support so 'ruthless' a candidate.

Professionally, Sinatra was climbing even higher, if that were possible for an entertainer already at the summit. He was nominated for seven Grammys, the recording industry award, and he won six of them. In June he gave eleven performances in nine days and earned over a million dollars.

That summer he began to use some of his audience-drawing ability to aid Humphrey's campaign. In August Frank drew a select audience of 700 at the Baltimore Civic Auditorium, singing at a $1,000-a-plate dinner for Humphrey supporters. Frank planned to make at least three similar appearances in other major cities for his candidate. But then the *Wall Street Journal* published a story headlined 'Sinatra's Pals', pointing out that the singer who was working so hard and so effectively for candidate Humphrey had demonstrated an enormous amount of loyalty to men like Giancana. Humphrey quietly cut Sinatra out of his campaign.

Frank soon gave up on the Democrats. He switched his allegiance to a Republican a couple of years after Nixon defeated Humphrey, supporting Ronald Reagan for governor of California in 1970 and campaigning strenuously for the politically conservative former actor. When Hollywood columnist Joyce Haber suggested that Sinatra had decided to help beat Reagan's Democratic opponent, Jesse Unruh, because Unruh had supported Bobby Kennedy in 1968, Frank called her to deny it.

'I'm supporting Reagan because he believes in what he does', Frank said. And he added, 'Now, Nixon *scares* me. He's running the country into the ground. I wouldn't be surprised if they dumped him in '72 ... Whatever the situation, the Democrats have got to get together and beat Nixon in '72.'

Nixon was apparently somewhat perturbed by Frank's criticism and decided to try and charm him. In September Frank flew down to Mexico in his private jet to attend a reception for President Diaz Ordaz as the special guest of President Nixon. Frank later told a columnist he was proud to have been the 'only Democrat' invited by Richard Nixon to an official function.

After Reagan was elected governor of California, he introduced Sinatra to Vice President Agnew and they soon became very fast friends; as has been pointed out, Sinatra's purely social relationship with Barbara Marx flowered into a romance because of their contact with Agnew. Slowly, Sinatra seemed to become a solid Republican and a White House insider with close personal contact with both the President and the Vice President. In the midst of his premature retirement, Frank entertained at the White House in April, 1973, and President Nixon suggested he should return to active entertaining. Sinatra said he'd consider it. A short time later Ole Blue Eyes was back, as his press agents put it.

Sinatra has said he came out of retirement because he was bored, because he missed the interplay and the sparks he gets in working with an audience. But some of his close friends have speculated that he returned to the stage mostly because of the disgrace which befell his good friend Agnew, forced to resign from office as a rather cheap crook. 'Frank had a lot invested in that friendship', a member of his circle has said, 'and the feeling is that he came back to entertainment because he wanted to show he wasn't going to be down after what they did to Agnew.'

Sinatra has sometimes blamed the press for Agnew's disgrace, as he often blames reporters and publicity-hungry politicians for all the attention devoted to his friendship with mobsters. Although Sinatra has a propensity for blaming others for problems he himself creates, it is plain beyond dispute that Frank has certainly been vilified on occasion by politicians trying to seize headlines and by the journalists who provide those headlines.

For example, in 1969 and early 1970, the New Jersey Crime Commission demanded that Frank appear before it and testify about his knowledge of local Mafia figures. Sinatra sent word that he had testified before several official bodies in the past and had been unable to assist any inquiries because his knowledge was limited, and he said he would be glad to testify in New Jersey in an executive session. The commission, knowing full well from FBI and other law enforcement agency reports that Sinatra didn't have any useful information about his friends' criminal activities, pressed ahead for its headlines and insisted that Frank must testify in public. Sinatra's lawyers tried to persuade the commission to soften its attitude, and the commission had Frank cited for contempt. One member admitted that Frank had been singled out because the agency wanted to prove it had the power to compel anyone to appear before it and not because Sinatra would have contributed any useful information. Another commission member told reporters, off the record, that it was trying to capture headlines by getting Sinatra on the witness stand. Frank did finally appear before the agency and testified for an hour. He answered all questions. The contempt charges were dropped.

In July, 1973, Sinatra again received a large amount of publicity when Senator Henry Jackson, a potential candidate for the presidency in 1976 and chairman of a Senate investigations committee, announced that he was looking into President Nixon's very curious release from Federal prison of a Mafia man. The *Mafioso* was Angelo (Gyp) DeCarlo, the 70-year-old leader of the New Jersey crime group, whose sentence had been commuted by President Nixon after he had served only two years of twelve on an extortion conviction. Members of Jackson's staff quietly and anonymously told reporters they had evidence that Frank Sinatra had used his influence with Agnew and Nixon to engineer DeCarlo's premature commutation. For days the headlines shouted the news of the 'Sinatra link' in the freeing of DeCarlo and buried the explanation that the mobster had been freed because he was dying of cancer. Then the stories simply vanished. Months later, buried on the back pages of all newspapers that bothered to report it, were small-type stories reporting that the FBI, after an extensive investigation, had failed to turn up 'one iota' of evidence suggesting there was anything improper in DeCarlo's release or that Sinatra had even known about it in advance. At around the same time, DeCarlo did die of cancer.

'Those stories really hurt Frank', the friend says. 'Making it appear that Frank got Agnew to get the President to release DeCarlo got to him in a bad way. Then when Agnew was kicked out of office – well, it goes together to explain why Frank came out of retirement. He just couldn't lay back and appear to be afraid to fight.'

Sinatra wrote a brief essay for the *New York Times* in 1972, after he was forced to testify before another official body, the Congressional Committee on Crime. Frank summed up how he felt about the 'politics of fantasy', as he termed the nature of the attacks on him. He wrote:

I answered all charges to the best of my ability. Assuming that the committee even needed the information, it was apparent to most people there that the whole matter could have been resolved in the privacy of a lawyer's office, without all the attendant hoopla.

But there are some larger questions raised by that appearance which have something to say to all of us. The most important is the rights of a private citizen in this country when faced with the huge machine of the central government. In theory, congressional investigating committees are fact-finding devices which are supposed to lead to legislation. In practice, as we learned during the ugly era of Joe McCarthy, they can become star chambers in which 'facts' are confused with rumour, gossip, and innuendo, and where reputations and character can be demolished in front of the largest possible audiences.

Sitting at the table the other day ... I wondered if the people out there in America knew how dangerous the whole proceeding was. My privacy had been robbed from me, I had lost hours of my life, I was being forced to defend myself in a place that was not even a court of law ... if this sort of thing could happen to me, it could happen to anyone, including those who cannot defend themselves properly.

EPILOGUE

Sinatra has now entered his swinging sixties and he will, he promises, be around for another quarter-century, still casting a giant shadow. 'In the year 2000', he said during an interview a couple of weeks before his sixtieth birthday, 'I'm going to give the biggest birthday party you've ever seen. Maybe in the Rome Colosseum. Maybe in the middle of Manhattan island. But I'll be here for the new century.'

So here is Frank Sinatra. Even if he is not yet in the September of his years, only the fools pretend to understand him; only the fools try to pin him down as one would a specimen in a display cabinet and affix a label on it: romantic, psychotic, childish.

But I will play the fool. It is so common an affliction among those who write about Sinatra that, in the end, I must succumb to the fool-virus.

Years ago, watching Sinatra-Maggio on the screen during the first run of *Eternity*, before the Oscar had been won, it suddenly occurred to me that this man I had idolized as a child had, like Rimbaud, although without Rimbaud's intense deliberateness, sought to reach down to the chaos that exists deep within all our natures. For Sinatra, the journey into that essential core of chaos had been his self-destructive pursuit of Ava Gardner and all the concomitant rages that went with it. And in the death of Maggio, up there on the screen, I felt the death of Sinatra – a catharsis, a purging of Sinatra as the emaciated, powerless, underdog drifter who loses again and again in life and in death. He had touched bottom, had Sinatra, and I felt he would never be down again because he had gained an inner strength from the descent.

What was happening to me in that darkened theatre, what has happened to so many of us caught up in Frank Sinatra – even those who did not become aware of his presence until they had gone through the Beatles and the rest – is that we were almost hypnotized by Sinatra's *space*. Like all entertainers, Sinatra creates his own space. But for most performers that space is usually limited to the stage, to film or television, to the domination of a specific audience. Sinatra's space has always been filled by the man, by the way he wishes us to perceive him, sometimes generous, sometimes irrational, occasionally destructive – but at all times a space filled by a man of Olympian proportions. His space has touched us all because in many ways Sinatra has seemed a heroic figure, forcing us to come to terms with a man who has defined in advance the way in which we must approach him, forcing us to recognize and applaud in him the essential chaos within us all, the chaos which few of us have the courage to face in ourselves.

There exists in all of us a being who, as G. K. Chesterton has described him, 'has no name, and all true tales of him are blotted out; yet he walks behind us in every forest path and wakes within us when the wind wakes at night. He is the origins – he is the man in the forest.' This, the so-called primitive 'evil' which has been civilized out of most of us and suppressed by our Judaic-Christian straitjackets, has been laid bare by Frank Sinatra. And simply by refusing to be anything but himself, in touch with his most primal emotions, Sinatra has become a surrogate for and a symbol of our own instinctive violent natures which have been socialized and bleached out of consciousness but which still struggle for release.

Like all great artists, whether singers or painters or poets, Sinatra is unable to evict the primitive childlike creature which is within him. And we, who had been required to deny the violent fantasizing child-force in order to exist in an 'adult' world, are temporarily reunited with that child in us because of the child in Sinatra. When Frank Sinatra punches an annoying restaurant patron or calls a columnist a two-dollar cunt, the men of reason among us condemn him. But the vast majority secretly applauds him and envies him and loves him for it. For who among us, reasonable and sober men and women, have not sometimes wished to act in a similarly decisive and violent manner?

But when all the biographical material and pop psychology is forgotten, when you're alone in front of a fire or in the midst of a noisy party and Sinatra's voice comes out of the speakers, singing the line from 'I'm a Fool to Want You', singing 'I love you' as only Sinatra can sing it, then you realize that Sinatra has always been correct: 'My personal life is my own business; all I owe you is my performance, my voice.'

Millions of words have been written about that voice, from the psychiatrist of the Forties sounding off in the newspapers that Frank was just a passing phenomenon accidentally filling a need for millions of women whose sons and lovers had gone off to fight a war, to intellectual musicologists writing of Sinatra's use of 'such age-old devices as slur, portamento, appoggiatura, mordent, and tempo rubato'. But Sinatra should be given the last word about that voice which has served him so well. He has said, at various times through the thirty-five years he has been quoted by writers and reporters, 'I used to listen to Jascha Heifetz on records, when I was starting to sing. His constant bowing, where you never heard a break, carried the melody line straight through, just like Dorsey's trombone. It was my idea to make my voice work in the same way as a trombone or violin – not sounding like them, but 'playing' the voice like those instruments.

'I remember once doing a benefit with a bunch of guys, and Benny Goodman was one of them. We were all boozing it up, but Benny was off in a corner noodling his clarinet. I went over to him and said, "Benny, every time I see you, you're practising." And he was – that man was never without his clarinet and he was always practising with it. When I asked him why, Benny said, "Purely because if I'm not great, if I can't be great, at least I'm going to be good." And it's true; I believe strongly in that as a singer. If you're working hard all the time, practising and working on your songs and you come to a slow period, maybe because of an emotional thing or you're just being lazy, then you're still very good even if you're not up to your top standard. You're still better than the other guy.

'There's something in your background, in my background – I try to transpose my thoughts about a song into a person who might actually be saying the words to someone. He's making his case. I don't know where it started, but I was doing it back with Tommy as a kid . . . I began to learn to use the lyric of a song as a script, as a dramatic scene.'

And finally, asked by an interviewer how he was able to so effectively communicate the mood of a song, Frank replied, 'It's because I get an audience involved, personally involved, in a song – because I'm involved myself . . . Being an 18-carat manic-depressive and having lived a life of violent emotional contradictions, I have an over-acute capacity for sadness as well as elation . . . Whatever else has been said about me personally is unimportant. When I sing, I believe. I'm honest . . . You can be the most artistically perfect performer in the world, but an audience is like a broad – if you're indifferent, endsville.'

All Sphere Books are available at your bookshop or newsagent, or can be ordered from the following address: Sphere Books, Cash Sales Department, P.O. Box 11, Falmouth, Cornwall.

Please send cheque or postal order (no currency), and allow 19p for postage and packing for the first book plus 9p per copy for each additional book ordered up to a maximum charge of 73p in U.K.

Customers in Eire and B.F.P.O. please allow 19p for postage and packing for the first book plus 9p per copy for the next 6 books, thereafter 3p per book.

Overseas customers please allow 20p for postage and packing for the first book and 10p per copy for each additional book.